Caught in the Act

A Comedy

Trevor Cowper

A Samuel French Acting Edition

SAMUELFRENCH-LONDON.CO.UK
SAMUELFRENCH.COM

Copyright © 1982 by Trevor Cowper
All Rights Reserved

CAUGHT IN THE ACT is fully protected under the copyright laws of the British Commonwealth, including Canada, the United States of America, and all other countries of the Copyright Union. All rights, including professional and amateur stage productions, recitation, lecturing, public reading, motion picture, radio broadcasting, television and the rights of translation into foreign languages are strictly reserved.

ISBN 978-0-573-11139-6

www.samuelfrench-london.co.uk

www.samuelfrench.com

FOR AMATEUR PRODUCTION ENQUIRIES

UNITED KINGDOM AND WORLD EXCLUDING NORTH AMERICA

plays@SamuelFrench-London.co.uk

020 7255 4302/01

Each title is subject to availability from Samuel French,

depending upon country of performance.

CAUTION: Professional and amateur producers are hereby warned that *CAUGHT IN THE ACT* is subject to a licensing fee. Publication of this play does not imply availability for performance. Both amateurs and professionals considering a production are strongly advised to apply to the appropriate agent before starting rehearsals, advertising, or booking a theatre. A licensing fee must be paid whether the title is presented for charity or gain and whether or not admission is charged.

The professional rights in this play are controlled by MacNaughton Lord 2000 Ltd, 44 S Molton St, London W1K 5RT.

No one shall make any changes in this title for the purpose of production. No part of this book may be reproduced, stored in a retrieval system, or transmitted in any form, by any means, now known or yet to be invented, including mechanical, electronic, photocopying, recording, videotaping, or otherwise, without the prior written permission of the publisher. No one shall upload this title, or part of this title, to any social media websites.

The right of Trevor Cowper to be identified as author of this work has been asserted by him in accordance with Section 77 of the Copyright, Designs and Patents Act 1988

CAUGHT IN THE ACT

First presented by Bill Kenwright and Charles Ross at the Theatre Royal, Norwich on 16th June, 1981. Subsequently transferring to the Garrick Theatre, London, on 4th September, 1981, with the following cast of characters

Cherry Winters	Judy Geeson
Cedric Travers	Geoffrey Colville
Martin Barclay	Martin Jarvis
Bill Taylor	Peter Blythe
Helen Temple	Helen Gill
Prince Hassan	Michael Walker

The play directed by Charles Ross
Setting by Alan Miller Bunford

The action takes place over several months in Cherry's London *pied-à-terre* adjoining her offices

Time—the present

ACT I
Scene 1

The set is a composite one, allowing the action of the play to flow freely. The main area (area 1) is Cherry's smart pied-à-terre, which occupies most of the centre of the stage. To one side (area 2) is a corridor with a front door into Cherry's flat, a door into Helen's flat opposite, and upstage a lift door. To the other side (area 3) is Cherry's office, with a communicating door. A further door leads off this to the other offices. Upstage doors lead from the main room to the kitchen and the bathroom

The furniture is good, modern and functional. In area 1 is a bed which folds back into a sofa. There is an easy chair in the room, also a coffee-table, a small dining-table with two chairs, bookshelves with a cupboard below: on top of the cupboard are drinks and glasses

When the CURTAIN *rises Cherry is lounging on the bed in her dressing-gown, reading. She is an attractive, feminine, highly independent and successful business executive*

Mr Travers enters the office, switches on the light, and sits at the desk with a file of papers. He is an older, somewhat weary director of Cherry's company, who tries to keep the ship steady, but has some unexpected hidden depths. After a moment he gets up to look for something in the upstage filing cabinet

Cherry, hearing a noise, goes to the office door and listens for a moment. She opens the door, not seeing Travers behind it

Travers (*popping his head round*) Hallo Cherry.

Cherry jumps

Cherry Mr Travers! (*Feeling her chest*) I think my heart just stopped. What are you doing at this hour?
Travers We have a crisis and I thought I'd prepare some figures for us to go through tomorrow morning.
Cherry Very conscientious of you. I had the same thoughts. Come in. (*She leads him into the flat and gives him her file of papers*) We have a cash-flow problem.
Travers Ah! Thank you. Yes, we've been overtrading. We need to inject more capital to expand—and rather quickly before our friendly bank manager turns nasty.
Cherry And yet our turnover is tremendous—confusing isn't it? And we're finding new markets. I hope Bill has done well in Tokyo.
Travers He's due back tomorrow isn't he?

Cherry Tonight actually. I suppose he'll wake me up.

Travers blushes. She smiles

Sorry if I've embarrassed you, Mr T.
Travers Not at all. After all, he is your fiancé.
Cherry (*vaguely*) Yes. I suppose he is really.
Travers You've always been so good at keeping your private life out of the office. So detached—it's a great gift.
Cherry Sometimes I wonder.
Travers When I have any problems with Dorothy, everyone knows about it.
Cherry Nonsense. Nothing seems to upset you.
Travers Don't you believe it. There's a lot of inner turmoil. That time little Willis dug up my prize chrysanths . . .
Cherry Willis?
Travers Her dog. She had three—Freeman and Hardy died, only Willis survives. I'm afraid I really lost my cool. By the way, I've got one of our new products to show you. (*He produces a brochure*)
Cherry Not *now*, Mr Travers. Anyway, I leave all that to you.
Travers Won't take a second. (*He indicates the brochure*) This is "Monique". Isn't she beautiful? She's life size and self inflated.
Cherry Why is she dressed like that?
Travers She's French. If you press her here, she says "*Oui, oui*". We were offered a gross of the Russian version that says "*Niet*", but I didn't think there'd be much demand.
Cherry How's she doing?
Travers We've introduced her into the West End branch last week and she outsold even the three-tailed plastic whips in the Bondage Department.
Cherry (*with a shrug*) *Vive le sport.* (*Frowning*) I often wonder how I ever got into this business.
Travers Through your far-sighted late husband, whose genius gave birth to the idea and look how it's grown already—fifteen branches.
Cherry Yes.
Travers You must never forget, dear madam chairperson, that we are providing a public service.
Cherry Dear Mr Travers, I do admire your confidence, but I doubt that everyone would appreciate our self-sacrificing spirit.
Travers We are taking sex off the streets and putting it back in the bedroom where it belongs.
Cherry Yes, well I must get some sleep, bring the figures with you in the morning, will you.
Travers Good night. I'll lock up.

Travers locks the office door, switches off the light and exits

Cherry goes to her front door and lifts the latch, then slips into bed and switches off the lamp. The flat is in almost complete darkness, save for a faint light in the corridor. There is a Musical Link

Act I, Scene 1

The lift door opens. An obviously weary figure, Martin, approaches the door of the flat. He fumbles for his key and, as he goes to put it in the lock the door swings open. Puzzled he shrugs his shoulders then tiptoes in. He is a barrister with political aspirations and fortunately a sense of humour; a bit pompous and sometimes charming

He undresses swiftly but silently in the gloom and then climbs into bed. The figure in bed half turns, moans sleepily and extends a welcoming arm

There is a fade to Black-out and a Musical Interlude, which reaches crescendo —typical film music with crashing waves for a comic effect. As the sound of implied intimacy recedes, daylight filters into the room and we observe two figures asleep in the bed. An alarm clock rings

Cherry switches it off and gets out of bed. Martin pulls the covers over his head and groans. Cherry moves upstage and notices an article of Martin's clothing which is lying on the floor. She bends to pick up the pair of trousers. She stops, examines the article closely, puzzled. She glances over at the bed and then back at the clothing. She hurriedly opens the curtains and studies the trousers again. A terrible, incredible thought crosses her mind. She goes over to the chair and picks up the jacket draped over it. She extracts the wallet from the jacket pocket, glances briefly inside it and then stands transfixed, her worst fears confirmed. Horrified, she moves towards the bed, checks herself, looks round for a suitable weapon. She picks up a bottle and holding it above her head in a threatening gesture she edges reluctantly over to the still sleeping figure. Gingerly, she lifts the covers and peers down at Martin. She utters a sharp little cry and starts back. Then, as though mesmerized, she edges back again and studies Martin's sleeping face. Having decided he is not unattractive and does not have any criminal traits—at least none that are visible—she relaxes a little. Enough to perceive some humour in the situation. After a slight hesitation, she prods the figure awake. Martin opens an eye and beams seraphically

Martin (*sleepily*) 'Morning darling. (*He mumbles*) What a night!
Cherry (*tapping her foot*) Yes.
Martin (*eyes still closed*) I'm exhausted. (*He opens one eye*) Oh, you've gone blonde. Nice. (*He settles down, eyes closed again*)
Cherry I've always been blonde.
Martin (*complacently*) Well, it suits you. I like blondes. They stimulate me.
Cherry Yes, I noticed.
Martin Oh, did you? Thank you. (*He opens his eyes*) Ohmigod! Who are you? (*There is a pause while he stares at her in amazement. Then he sits up with a rush, as if to get up*)
Cherry (*raising the bottle menacingly*) Stay where you are!
Martin (*with dignity, pulling the bedclothes round his neck*) I assure you I'm not going to attack you. I haven't got any clothes on!

Cherry raises her eyes to the ceiling

Cherry I suppose you can explain what you're doing in my bed?
Martin Your bed?

Cherry (*firmly*) My bed.
Martin Then where's Helen's bed?
Cherry Underneath Helen, I imagine, wherever she may be.
Martin But she was here. Last night we—er—I—er—er . . .
Cherry (*deliberately*) Not to her. To me.
Martin Oh God—there's been a terrible mistake!
Cherry Was it *so* terrible?
Martin No! No! I mean—no. I . . . I must go! (*He flings back the bedclothes, remembers he is naked and sits back groaning*)
Cherry Was there something?
Martin My—(*looking around for his clothes*)—pants.
Cherry Ah, yes. (*She folds her arms*)

Martin sees his pants on the floor near the bottom of the bed and dives down to retrieve them by stretching an arm out from under the bedclothes. He finally locates them and struggles to put them on under the cover. Cherry watches him

You're not very good at that. You should get more practice.

Martin finally emerges, presumably panted

Martin (*pathetically*) Where am I?
Cherry In a strange bed in Sloane Mansions.
Martin Number forty-five?
Cherry Getting warmer. Forty-six.
Martin (*after a long pause, with a false laugh*) Oh well—a miss is as good as a mile.
Cherry (*icily*) You *didn't* miss.
Martin And—er—forty-five?
Cherry Across the way. No—don't tell me, let me guess—Heather?
Martin Helen. How did I end up here?
Cherry I'd say you turned left instead of right.
Martin Ohmigod. You see I've never been here—there before. Helen has only just moved in.
Cherry The tall, rather languid lady?
Martin That's her—do you know her?
Cherry Intimately. She's had a pint of gold top and a small yoghurt every day this week.
Martin (*reflectively*) Yes. She's got a marvellous complexion. (*He thinks something over*)
Cherry Has she?
Martin Of course! All this; it's a joke, isn't it?
Cherry (*looking around at the decor*) Well—it's the best I could do on a limited budget . . .
Martin No, I mean you've been put up to it.
Cherry Go on.
Martin Well, how was I able to walk straight in? How come your door wasn't locked?

Pause. Cherry shrugs

Act I, Scene 1

Aha! I've got you there, haven't I? The middle of the night and the door not locked. Ha!
Cherry I can explain . . .
Martin (*interrupting her in his triumph*) Helen actually *does* live here. She slipped out early this morning and let you in!
Cherry Why on earth should she do that?
Martin To pay me back in some way, I suppose, for forgetting her birthday or something. Just like her.
Cherry (*shaking her head to indicate how wrong he is*) That's not very loyal of you.
Martin Well if I'm not right, what about you? Leaving your door unlocked so that strange men can wander in at all hours of the night and—well why was it open, anyway?
Cherry Bill.
Martin Aha! Bill! All is revealed at last. (*Pause*) Who's Bill?
Cherry My—er—fiancé—Bill Taylor.
Martin Oh. And he's a midget—he can't reach the lock.
Cherry He's over six foot.
Martin Oh—ohhh . . .
Cherry His plane was due in from Tokyo in the early hours of the morning.
Martin Oh.
Cherry He's obviously been delayed.

Pause. They stare at each other

Just as well, really.
Martin For both of us. (*Pause*) I mean it could have been awkward.
Cherry Yes. He used to play full-back for the Army.
Martin I imagine. (*Pause*) Keeps pretty fit still, I suppose.
Cherry Hard as iron. Solid muscle.
Martin I really must be going.
Cherry Yes. I think you must.

They look at each other. The barriers are down at last

Martin Please understand. I'm so sorry. I'd been driving down from the Midlands and I was tired and—er . . .
Cherry (*with a hint of a smile*) Not *too* tired.
Martin No. But this is *terrible*. (*He continues dressing under the sheet*)

Bill is seen coming out of the lift. He is a director of Cherry's firm and her lover: ex-army, humourless and well-built, with an unfortunate stutter under stress

Cherry Not all that terrible—but it will be when he arrives.
Martin Oh, Lord, yes—George.
Cherry Bill.

The figure in the corridor presses the bell. Martin freezes in horror with the bedclothes pulled up round his neck

Martin Oh. God!

Cherry (*calmly, but whispering*) No. Probably Bill. You'd better hurry. He's bigger than you are, and has no sense of humour at all. Please hide!

Martin leaps up, collecting his clothes

Martin (*rushing towards a door upstage*) Where's the bathroom?
Cherry (*whispering loudly*) That's no good, he's bound to want to use it. I mean he's come all the way from Tokyo. (*She points to the wardrobe*) Try in there.
Martin That's ridiculous. First place he'd look.
Cherry He's not actually *expecting anyone* to be here.
Martin (*indicating the office door*) What's in here?
Cherry That's no good, it's locked.

Bill, in the corridor, continues to press the bell, then shouts

Bill Hey, Winters—it's me.
Martin (*pausing in his search for somewhere to hide*) Winters?
Cherry (*picking up Martin's clothes from the floor*) He calls me Winters. It's my surname. (*She calls*) Coming!
Martin Oh, I see. Silly of me.
Bill (*outside the door*) Well get a move on, old girl. It's long past reveille.

Martin, in desperation, rolls under the bed

Cherry Good idea! Don't panic. I'll get rid of him. (*She quickly thrusts the rest of Martin's clothes under the bed after him except for one shoe, then moves towards the front door, pausing to stretch luxuriously and yawn*) Coming, darling!

She opens the front door. Bill grins and enters, like a wrestler in search of prey

Bill (*putting down an overweight suitcase*) Dammit, Winters, I thought you said you'd leave the door on the latch.
Cherry Oh, I'm sorry, Bill—I thought I had.
Bill (*generously*) Probably just as well. You never know these days ...
Cherry (*looking anxiously towards the bed*) No.
Bill (*holding out his arms*) Winters!
Cherry (*smiling but staying where she is*) Taylor!
Bill You look marvellous. (*He stutters a bit when he gets emotional or angry*) When—W-winters c-comes—can Spring be far behind? (*He laughs at his own joke and before Cherry can answer, picks her up bodily and carries her over to the bed. He drops her on it fairly unceremoniously, kneels over her and kisses her*)
Cherry (*weakly*) Oh, Bill!
Bill Winters!
Cherry (*pushing him off*) Darling, it's awfully late—I mean early.
Bill (*taking off his jacket*) I know. Sorry, I was so late. Bloody plane was delayed. I've been thinking about you all the way from Tokyo.
Cherry (*grasping at a straw*) And how *was* Tokyo?
Bill Oh, great. But that can wait until the morning.

Act I, Scene 1

Cherry Darling—it *is* the morning.
Bill I mean the office.
Cherry (*edging into a slightly more decorous position*) Oh, but I want to know now. Any hope for our products?

Cherry carefully stands in front of the bed. Bill drops his tie and she bends down as he bends to pick it up. Bill is confused

Bill I say, old girl, are you totally A-One? You haven't gone off me?
Cherry No, darling—but—well—I am rather tired.
Bill You're due for a spot of leave. You work too hard Winters—and summers too for that matter. (*Kneeling over her*) Mustn't let things get on top of you.
Cherry Well I'm trying not to . . .

Bill undoes his belt

Oh! Bill, do let's save it up for later.
Bill Save it up for later—I've been saving it so long I'm drawing interest!

Bill starts unzipping his trousers and Cherry, with horror on her face, grabs Bill's arm

Cherry Bill, I'm awfully late and I've got Hardacre coming at nine to discuss New York.
Bill Oh, Hardacre. I'd forgotten. Well you carry on. I'll join you in the office—and as we are not going to use it I'll fold the bed up for you.
Cherry (*wildly*) Don't worry about that . . .
Bill No trouble.
Cherry Leave it! I'm—er—going to change the sheets.

Too late. Bill with an effortless flourish has folded the bed back into a sofa to reveal the recumbent Martin, half dressed, trying to look nonchalant. He smiles up at Bill hopefully. There is a long pause

Martin Good morning.
Bill (*surprisingly normal*) What's this m-m-man doing here?

Cherry smiles weakly and shrugs her shoulders as if to say: "I-don't-know-what-he's-doing-there-either"

Cherry I can't conceive.
Martin (*aside*) Thank God for that!
Bill Who are y-y-you?
Martin Barclay—Kumfybed Company. Miss Winters has been having trouble with her springs.
Bill I don't think I believe you. That's not a Kumfybed—that's a Sleepezee. Stand up, you swine!

Martin gets slowly to his feet and musters as much dignity as vest, one sock and underpants permit

Martin (*very normal*) Good morning. I can explain everything . . .
Bill I don't know w-what you're doing, but you shouldn't be doing it here.

Martin It's really perfectly straightforward . . .
Bill Silence—when you speak to me!
Martin Oh, right . . .

Bill grabs him by the neck and propels him towards the front door. He opens it and pushes Martin through

(*Turning*) Could I have my clothes, please?

Bill punches Martin in the face and slams the door

(*Reeling from the blow*) But I'll catch cold. (*He shouts at the door*) I'll be arrested! I'll be disbarred!

Bill picks up some of Martin's clothes and throws them into the passage where Martin picks them up and starts to dress, nervously looking at Helen's door. Bill turns on Cherry

Cherry withdraws rapidly to the bathroom and slams the door

Bill Winters—open this door! I demand an explanation.
Cherry (*off*) You wouldn't believe it.
Bill Come on, Winters—open up! I mean—dammit.
Cherry (*off*) Go away! I'm upset.
Bill Well, I'm upset too. I mean, dammit! I come back from Tokyo, f-f-f-find you totally unresponsive—and then f-f-find a strange man in his knickers, under your bed—how d'you think I f-f-feel? (*Pause*) I'm sh-sh-sh—
Cherry (*off*) Oh, shut up!
Bill I'm s-speechless, that's what I am. I order you to open the door!
Cherry (*off*) You're not one of the army any more and I'm not one of your privates.
Bill Don't be absurd. I haven't got any privates.

Outside Cherry's flat, Martin continues dressing

The door to the next-door flat opens and Helen stands glaring at him. She is Martin's very upper-class, laconic and good-looking fiancée, the daughter of the man whose company has briefed Martin and who also could be beneficial to his political ambitions. She wears a dressing-gown and has clearly been woken up by the noise. She is exquisite looking, and speaks in an affected, drawly and expressionless voice

Helen Do you usually dress in the corridor?
Martin (*casually hopping on one leg as he puts on a sock*) Oh hello, darling.
Helen I was expecting you last night.
Martin I know, I—er—missed the turning.

Bill gives up banging on the door, paces across the bedroom, trips over Martin's shoe and coat, picks them up and flings them into the passage and closes the door

Oh, thank you.
Helen (*deadpan*) What's in there? A dry cleaners?

Act I, Scene 1

Martin Helen, you're not going to believe this, I know, but . . .

While Martin is speaking, Bill goes and bangs on the bathroom door and he and Martin speak together

Bill Winters—out here—explain!

Cherry enters into the lounge and she and Martin speak together

Martin (*to Helen*) I was most frightfully tired, you see, having driven all the way from Birmingham—and the traffic was *unbelievable*, darling—four abreast on the M1—*huge* juggernauts, all crawling along, it was absolutely *mind-bending*. And when I got here, absolutely *drunk* with fatigue, I simply took the wrong turning and flopped into the first bed that crossed my path—and it happened to have this girl in it, you see, who, of course, I thought was you, but actually I'd never seen her before in my life. . . .

Cherry Very well. (*To Bill*) There was I—fast asleep—absolutely exhausted after a perfectly foul day—I'd had three hours with the accountants and you *know* what that means. And suddenly I was woken up—well, not suddenly, really, it was very gradual and gentle and actually, of course I wasn't properly awake at all—by this man creeping into bed beside me and I thought: "Ooh, how lovely—it's Bill" and sort of dropped off again but, of course, it wasn't you, how was I to know that? And that's the absolute truth. I swear it, but of course, I can't expect you to believe it. Now I'm going to have a shower.

Cherry goes into the bathroom

Bill What . . . ? Right! I'm going, Winters, since you clearly consider your ablutions more important than our continuing relationship. Winters!—*I'm going . . .*

Cherry (*off*) All right! Go!

Bill Perhaps it may not be too much to expect a proper explanation when you've—sh-sh-sho- . . .

Cherry (*off*) Oh, shut up!

Bill I haven't finished yet. When you've . . . (*He tails off*) Oh—(*he mutters*) —I can't remember what I w-w-was going to say . . .

Bill crosses to the front door which he flings open. Immediately we pick up the conversation of Martin and Helen

Martin Why won't you listen?

Bill (*muttering to himself*) Thinks she can muck about with any Tom, Dick or—H-H-Harr- . . .

Martin My name's Martin.

Bill socks Martin on the jaw. Martin slumps to the floor and holds his jaw

Ow!

Bill (*to Helen*) If he's yours, madam, you should put bromide in his tea. He's a sex maniac.

Bill turns on Martin, aims to sock him on the jaw again but Martin ducks and Bill hits the wall. He stumps off

Ouch!
Helen (*calling after him*) Well done, sir—whoever you are!

Bill bows politely, and gets into the lift, rubbing his sore fist

(*Nodding towards Cherry's door*) Who's in there?
Martin (*struggling to his feet*) I don't know. She didn't tell me her name.
Helen (*still amazingly deadpan*) I think it's *awfully* mean of you!
Martin Darling, I . . .
Helen I could hit you!

Helen gives Martin a resounding smack on the face and slams her door

Martin stands in the corridor indecisively for a moment then realizes he is still missing a shoe and rings the bell of Cherry's flat

Cherry comes out of the bathroom

Cherry (*shouting*) Go away!

Martin continues to ring the bell and Cherry, exasperated, goes to open it

(*Angrily*) Well? (*She sees it is Martin and recoils*) Oh, no!
Martin I'm sorry—I seem to be missing a shoe.

Cherry stands aside and motions him in, rather apprehensively, as if doubtful of what he is going to do this time. Martin makes a rush towards the sofa/bed and Cherry leaps out of the way

It's obviously here somewhere—ah, here it is.

He picks it up and stands facing her, awkwardly. Neither knows what to say Finally, they speak in a rush, simultaneously

Martin⎫ You know I really don't know what—sorry. ⎧(*Speaking*
Cherry⎭ I suppose this is really quite funny—sorry ⎩ *together*)
Cherry⎫
Martin⎭ I don't want you to think—sorry. (*Speaking together*)
Cherry (*with a suggestion of a smile*) You first.
Martin (*looking at her with glowing admiration*) I'm—er—lost for words.
Cherry You know—I don't sleep with many people but I do make a point of knowing their names.
Martin Of course, I'm so sorry—Martin Barclay—barrister. You are very direct, aren't you?
Cherry Do I shock you?
Martin Not exactly, but I do come from a long line of vicars.
Cherry Then you should understand the frailties of the flesh.
Martin Oh, I do—frequently.
Cherry Barclay—barrister. Haven't I read something about you?
Martin You may have done, I had a little success not so long ago with Lord Carbridges anti-porn clean-up Soho campaign. I was prosecuting counsel.
Cherry I remember now. (*Puzzled by his black coat and striped trousers*) Vicars. Is that why you wear those funny clothes?

Martin No. These are just the badge of my calling. In America I can wear jeans. Here they expect you to look like an undertaker. When in Rome—
Cherry —do as the Romans do and rape the women.
Martin That's unfair—even the Sabines kicked and screamed a bit, just for the look of it. (*Wistfully*) My Sabine was rather supine.
Cherry Oh. (*Pause*) That's unfair—(*faltering a little and turning away*)—I was tired, too. I didn't realize . . .
Martin Really? Not even a passing thought?
Cherry Well, it did occur to me that perhaps Bill has been practising . . .
Martin I think that's the nicest thing anyone's ever said to me. You mean he's—er—not very good at—er . . .
Cherry (*loyally*) Oh, no! He's fine, but he makes love rather like he plays cricket—stylish but predictable. And you?
Martin (*quietly*) Oh, I don't play cricket.
Cherry Good! I mean—didn't you notice anything?
Martin Of course not. I wouldn't have dreamed of taking advantage of you if I'd even suspected . . .
Cherry You mean I'm just a carbon copy of dear old—Hester—next door?
Martin Helen. No, of course not.
Cherry Didn't you enjoy it?
Martin (*very sincerely*) It was marvellous. Unbelievable. Like a dream.
Cherry (*looking pleased*) Would you like some coffee? (*She goes towards the kitchen door*)
Martin Very much. Thank you.
Cherry Actually I'm not often here—only when I work late at the office, next door. Normally, I commute from Sussex.

Cherry exits to the kitchen

Martin I suppose the only thing I can do is to apologize.

No reply. He continues practising apologies to himself while he straightens his tie and hair

"I'm most awfully sorry, Miss Winters—I seem, quite inadvertently, to have stumbled into your flat uninvited—and committed the most apalling intimacy . . ." No. "Miss Winters, I never have been able to find my way in the dark . . ." No. (*Softly*) "The fact remains, Miss Winters—that you are very attractive—the sort of girl I could go for—my type . . ."
Cherry (*off*) Black or white?
Martin (*still thinking of his type*) Oh, white—mostly. (*He shouts*) I mean, white. Thank you. (*He looks at his watch*) Oh! My God I'm late for Lord Temple . . . (*He is now in a dilemma—wanting to stay and needing to leave*).
Cherry (*off*) What are you muttering about?
Martin I was just apologizing . . .
Cherry What for?

Cherry enters with a coffee tray

Martin Well—er—you know—for . . .

Cherry "Violating" me?

Martin (*sheepishly*) What can I say?

Cherry (*putting the tray down*) Look, you stumbled in here by a fluke and had it away with a totally strange woman. Right? And now you don't want to talk about it. With me. You're embarrassed. You'd "ho-ho" about it for hours with your male friends, wouldn't you? "You'll never guess what happened to me, folks, on my way back from Manchester . . ."

Martin Birmingham. (*He looks at his watch*)

Cherry Birmingham. Well it happened. I accept it. I accept that some single lady who has moved in opposite, who apparently, is accustomed to receiving you, at all hours, in total silence and on whom you homed last night, like a sleepy but oversexed pigeon—only to find it was the wrong nest. I accept it. I'm not going to boast about it. But at least I don't mind talking about it. Directly. Objectively. Coffee? (*She hands him a cup*)

Martin Thank you. (*He thinks over what she has said*) Right. What specific aspect of it do you want to discuss?

Cherry I don't. It's just that you men are so old-fashioned. You insult a woman's intelligence. Why can't you be strong and free and fearlessly independent? And more important—why can't you be more flexible towards us women who want to be strong and free and fearlessly independent?

Martin On the contrary, I'm really very flexible. I'm flexible enough to be rigid or flexible, as the occasion demands.

Cherry Take Bill, for instance . . .

Martin Ah, Action Man . . .

Cherry Re-action man. He's part of the universal chauvinist club and has all the typical male orientated reflexes. Not prepared to listen for a moment to a perfectly logical and reasonable explanation—WHICH JUST HAPPENED TO BE TRUE—before jumping to the wrong conclusion!

Martin Look, I don't quarrel with many people but I do make a point of knowing their names.

Cherry (*laughing and holding out her hand*) Cherry Winters. Company Director.

Martin How do you do? Don't answer that! (*Pause*) Of course, you have to admit that both our explanations do suffer from a fundamental lack of integrity. I mean—while the burden of proof lies upon our respective lovers to produce evidence that we did *not* know we were *not* making love to them at the precise moment we were in fact making love to each other—the evidence that we were so doing is purely circumstantial.

Cherry You must be a very good lawyer—because I haven't the foggiest idea what you're talking about.

Martin That's what the Chairman of Midland Motors keeps telling me.

Cherry Lord Temple? What's he got to do with it?

Act I, Scene 1   13

Martin I'm retained by an American firm that's trying to take him over. They're hoping that an injection of U.S. methods, incentives, capital, and so on, may make Midland more viable. You know—American "know-how".
Cherry (*drily*) Well—you know how. Not where, but how. How's it going?
Martin Well—as you can imagine, there are political problems. Union opposition—questions in the House—too much American control of British Industry.
Cherry You sound very gloomy about it.
Martin (*shrugging his shoulders*) It's a personal thing, as well. I have what are called "political ambitions" and I've been adopted as the Conservatives' candidate for Bromwich South—which just happens to have most of Midland Motors component factories in it—
Cherry —so being identified with the dastardly foreign takeover is not exactly a plus with the voters? That's bad.
Martin Exactly. And Lord Temple—as well as being Chairman of British Midland happens to be Chairman of the Constituency branch of the Conservative Party—
Cherry But if he wants to be taken over, that's good?
Martin —but he also happens to be my fiancée's father . . .
Cherry What, old Doris opposite? That's bad.
Martin Helen.
Cherry Helen.
Martin Yes, so I am going to need all my powers of advocacy to retrieve the situation. Father may not take too kindly to his future son-in-law's —erratic—er . . .
Cherry Eroticism?
Martin Quite. (*He looks at his watch*) My God, I must be going. If you were Helen as it were, what would it take to bring *you* round?
Cherry (*smiling*) Well I'm different, remember. Objective, unemotional. I would accept a rational, honest, well-argued explanation. And when that failed—two dozen roses and a bottle of Dom Perignon delivered abjectly on all fours.
Martin I'll remember that. (*He gets up*)
Cherry I shouldn't rush over immediately.
Martin Good point. Give her time to calm down—think more rationally.
Cherry Er—yes. (*She takes the tray with the coffee things to kitchen*)
Martin I'll leave it till this evening. Well thanks.
Cherry My pleasure.

They move towards the door

Martin I'm so glad. Well, I don't suppose—since we're both happily involved with other people—you've got Fred—
Cherry —and you've got Mabel—
Martin —I don't suppose we'll be seeing each other again.
Cherry No—I suppose not.

They shake hands and Martin calls the lift

Martin Nice knowing you.
Cherry (*with her eyebrows slightly raised*) *So* glad you could come.

Martin exits to corridor and into the lift

Cherry closes the front door and exits to the bathroom

The Lights fade up on Area 3.

SCENE 2

A few moments later

Travers enters into the office and knocks on the flat door

Travers Cherry? (*He unlocks flat door*) Cherry, I'm in.
Cherry (*off*) Okay, Mr Travers I'll be with you in a minute.

The telephone rings

Travers (*on the telephone*) Travers here . . . No, I'm afraid Cherry's not in yet, Bill . . . Yes, she is a bit late—probably had a bad night, poor dear . . . Another man in the bed? . . . Bit of a crush wasn't it? . . . Oh I see, underneath . . . Well I don't want to know about that and it's really not for me to venture an opinion on our Chairperson's er—nocturnal inexactitude . . . Were you thinking of coming in today? . . . Well we are rather expecting your report. We didn't send you to Tokyo for the mixed bathing you know . . . No, I can't confine her to quarters, it's just not practical . . . Now calm down, Bill, and I'll tell Cherry that you'll be around about seven o'clock tonight . . . Good-bye, Bill. I'm so glad that Dorothy and I are getting too old for all that!

Travers exits out of the office

The Lights fade to a Black-out, then come up again immediately on Area 1.

SCENE 3

Cherry is tidying the flat

Bill enters from the kitchen

Bill I find your attitude absolutely extraordinary. I mean, you allow a strange man to spend the night in your room—in your bed—and take no more notice of him than if he'd come to read the meter! You know what you've done don't you, you've deliberately sabotaged our relationship!
Cherry (*icily calm but furious. As she talks she continues to move about the flat, tidying up*) Why, won't you even listen? That's what really annoys me. "My mind is made up, don't confuse me with the facts". That's your position. Why can't you . . .
Bill I've t-t-told you: I'm trying to keep an open mind . . .
Cherry Vacant is the word. Why can't you put aside your emotional involvement, look at the facts . . .

Act I, Scene 3   15

Bill (*interrupting*) The f-f-facts speak for themselves. I come home from Tokyo at f-four o'clock in the morning and f-f-find a half-dressed man under your bed. What am I supposed to think he's doing there—f-f-f-fixing a fuse? (*He fixes himself a drink*)
Cherry He had a date with his fiancée, who lives opposite; he was very tired, exhausted, having driven from Birmingham. I, expecting my sweet, itinerant, understanding lover from Tokyo, had gone to bed dog-tired; leaving the door on the latch; when, in the small hours of the morning, the expected male creeps gently into my bed in the dark, exhausted and expectant—but not too exhausted—we make love. Now, what could be more reasonable than that?
Bill But how can you expect me to believe—that you—that he—that I . . . ? Surely you must have n-n-noticed? I'm speechless. I really am. (*Bill sits down on the sofa*)
Cherry Speechless—how could I notice. We didn't speak. Besides, he's roughly the same size as you are.
Bill Oh my God!
Cherry Anyway I did notice—later.
Bill Well, it's finished—I can't go on like this—I'm a reasonable man—an extremely reasonable man—and that is something about which I will not argue! No—I can't go on like this—I mean I couldn't wait to get home from Tokyo—a matter of a few hours delay—I mean what if we'd been hi-jacked I ask myself! Oh no—finished—I'm leaving! (*He rises*)
Cherry All right, go! I'm sorry, but if only you weren't so damned dishonest! Why don't you admit it? It isn't that you don't believe that I'm being absolutely truthful about what happened, or that I was mistakenly made love to by a perfect stranger—that's not what's making you annoyed. It's because you suspect that I might have enjoyed it.

At this point the lift doors open at the end of the corridor and Martin emerges, carrying a huge bunch of flowers and a bottle of champagne. He walks slowly down the passage

Bill (*at the door*) My God, W-Winters, that's a pretty caddish thing to say!

Martin approaches Cherry's front door as if in a daze, realizes his mistake, shakes his head and turns towards Helen's door opposite. He rings the bell and waits

Cherry (*shouting at Bill*) I feel "*caddish*"! That's one of the side effects of being battered by the jolly old Bulldog Drummond approach for the last two years—
Bill Oh!

Bill retreats to the door, pursued by Cherry

Cherry —you make me feel like the captain of the opposing Rugger team!
Bill M-more like the hooker, if I may say so.

Bill goes out to the corridor

Cherry Oh! (*She opens the door and screams after him*) And I *did* enjoy it! (*She slams the door in his face. Then, very softly and sadly*) And I thought it was you. (*She goes back into her room and pours herself a drink*)

Bill glances at Martin, waiting for Helen's door to open. Martin holds the flowers up to his face and turns away

Bill continues down the corridor and exits via the lift. Helen's door opens and Helen looks unenthusiastically at Martin

Helen Oh, it's you.

Martin (*putting a brave face on it*) Of course it's me. Were you expecting someone else?

Helen (*deadpan*) Never know your luck.

Martin (*in a rush*) Darling, this is true confession time—I don't want you to—I mean, you've really got to believe that I didn't know it wasn't you in the bed.

Helen You said that before.

Martin But you're not listening ... I mean, you've hardly given me a fair hearing. Your mind was totally made up before I even arrived, wasn't it? You were determined not to listen to a word I had to say, weren't you?

Helen Yes. (*She struggles with the engagement ring on her finger*)

Martin Well, I think that's most unfair. After all we've meant to each other, all the glorious times we've had together, the laughter and tears, the *fun*—

Helen Oh, do belt up.

Helen finally gets her ring off, drops it on the floor, goes into her flat and slams the door

After a pause Martin gets down and finds the ring

Martin Fun? It was bloody awful! Like making love to a Dalek. (*He pauses for a moment, contemplating the roses and champagne he is still carrying—and rings the bell to Cherry's flat*)

Cherry sitting quietly with her stiff drink responds instantly. Thinking it is Bill she picks up a jug of water from the table, opens the door and flings the water at the offending visitor

Cherry Oh, it's you.

Martin stands dripping

Martin Don't tell me—you thought it was the Sandhurst full-back with the right hook. I just saw him leave. (*He looks over his shoulder*)

Cherry (*laughing*) Don't worry about Bill—he's his own worse enemy.

Martin Not while I'm around, he isn't.

Cherry You'd better come in.

Martin Are you sure? You can't be too careful.

Cherry Yes, I'm sure!

Cherry stands aside and Martin enters

Martin Oh, here . . . (*He hands Cherry the flowers*)
Cherry Oh, thank you. (*She takes the dripping roses*) I'll give them some water—you open the champagne.

Cherry exits to the kitchen with the roses

Martin That's what I like—instant decisions.

Martin starts to open the champagne

Meanwhile we see the lift doors open and Bill marches back down the corridor, frowning horribly. He hesitates at Cherry's door and rings on Helen's door

Helen's door opens and a teddy-bear flies out at him, some earlier gift from Martin, no doubt, when times were better

Helen (*off*) Bugger off!

Helen appears at the door

Oh.
Bill Oh, sorry—didn't mean to intrude but I thought I'd ask, are you engaged to that f-f-f-philanderer?
Helen I was.
Bill Sod there with the flowers and champagne?
Helen Yes.

Bill picks up the teddy-bear and looks at it

Bill Sort of swine who steals a girl's honour, then gives her a teddy bear.
Helen Yes.
Bill You know he spent the night with my girl.
Helen Really!
Bill God! I need a d-d-d-drink.
Helen So do I! (*She goes into her flat—returns*) Well come on, then!

Helen exits. Bill follows her in

Bill Oh, thanks, you forgot your teddy . . .

Cherry returns from the kitchen carrying the roses which she has put in a vase

Cherry They're lovely. Well how did the explanation go? Did you get down on all fours?
Martin Only to retrieve the ring. (*He opens the champagne*)
Cherry Oh! Poor you, I'm sorry.
Martin What about you?
Cherry I wish I'd had a ring to throw at Bill.

He hands her a glass

Martin In his present mood I'd put it through his nose!

They clink glasses and she eyes the bottle as she drinks

Cherry I'll drink to that!

The Lights fade to a Black-out

SCENE 4

One to three weeks later, suggesting a progression in their relationships, Bill and Helen enter from the lift

Bill Oh, Helen, I really enjoyed luncheon with your father, but I think I let you down, old girl.

Helen No. No, Daddy really enjoyed your army stories—but you weren't very polite about the pudding!

Bill Well how was I to know it was a blancmange in his regimental colours, I was pi—pi—preoccupied, thinking about that business last Friday—do you believe Martin?

Helen No.

Bill Nor do I. Do you believe Cherry?

Helen No.

Bill Nor do I. How could they expect us to believe them?

Helen Quite.

Bill I mean, how could one make a mistake like that—even in the dark—could *you*?

Helen No.

Bill Even if you were t-tired?

Helen I'm always tired.

Pause

Bill Really? It's the most obvious, clumsy, bare-faced lie—

Helen (*searching her bag for front door key*) Bizarre.

Bill (*after a pause*) —unless of course they're telling the truth.

Helen I don't really care any more. Can't we forget it? (*A long pause*) Of course if she didn't move very much he might have thought it was me ...

Helen and Bill exit into Helen's flat

The Lights fade to a Black-out, and rise in the lounge, where Martin and Cherry are just finishing a meal

Martin I'm glad that your strong opinions about the emancipated woman's role in society has not inhibited your culinary skills.

Cherry Does that mean you enjoyed the steak and kidney pud?

Martin Absolutely. Do compliments embarrass you?

Cherry So that's what it was!

Martin Sorry. It's my legal training. I always use six words when one will do. It puts up the fees.

Cherry Well you must eat here more often. (*She clears the plates*)

Martin I'd like to. You know we've known each other now—(*looking in his diary*)—for two weeks. But one of them doesn't count. You wouldn't see me.

Act I, Scene 4 19

Cherry I know. I'm sorry. I thought it best to give ourselves time to think. (*She sits on the couch*)
Martin Oh, I've been thinking all right!
Cherry Have you?
Martin Turning it over in my mind—distracting, rather disturbing thoughts.
Cherry Why disturbing?
Martin I was afraid the initial interaction was purely physical.
Cherry Well it was bound to be—since neither of us spoke a word.
Martin Precisely. Which is why we needed time. To talk and think.
Cherry And now?
Martin Now I'm fully convinced—there's something else. A great deal more. (*He moves down and stands behind the couch*) Cherry . . .
Cherry Yes?
Martin The circumstances of our meeting—I can hardly believe them myself—and I thought that maybe we could—well—just to prove that it wasn't a figment of the imagination—er—try it again.
Cherry I think we should—we might even talk a little.
Martin Well just the odd grunt of approval.

They embrace as the Lights fade and come up in the corridor

Bill comes out of Helen's flat door wearing only a dressing gown and looking tousled. He bends down and picks up a milk carton and newspaper. Opening the paper he casually reads the headlines

Helen (*off*) Darling.
Bill Coming d-d- . . . sweetheart.

Helen appears, also déshabillée

Helen (*kissing his cheek*) The bed is getting cold. (*Another kiss and a pause*) Is it very difficult?
Bill What?
Helen Seeing her in the office all the time.
Bill Who?
Helen Your boss.
Bill Well not lately—we haven't been out of this flat for three days.
Helen I think it would be nice if you gave it up.
Bill What after only three days?
Helen The business!
Bill What—the business? I can't afford to. It's a jolly good living.
Helen Why don't you go into Parliament? All my fiancés do.

Helen exits into her flat, followed by Bill

The Lights fade, and come up on Area 1

Martin and Cherry walk down from the kitchen and sit on the sofa

Cherry What do you want most out of life?

Martin They change, don't they—our ambitions? I don't remember ever going through the engine driver, fireman phase.
Cherry What do little boys want nowadays, I wonder?
Martin Little girls are popular I believe. When I was a boy I wanted to be an actor, to hold a discerning audience in the palm of my sticky little hand. I was a rotten show-off.
Cherry So you became a barrister instead?
Martin Exactly and the actor in me sways a discerning jury. When I was first called to the bar I wanted to be an Attorney General or Lord Chief Justice. Now—oh, a good living, a few really worthwhile cases—the power to influence events, the love of a good woman. And you?
Cherry I think I've got practically everything I've ever wanted. There's something in me that isn't satisfied by the usual feminine pursuits. I seem to need challenge, the uncertainties of business, independence of action ...
Martin And where did Bill fit into all that?
Cherry Jealous, darling?
Martin Not exactly, but it must be difficult seeing him in the office every day?
Cherry You must be joking, he hasn't been in for a week.
Martin Really? You know what I mean though.
Cherry Darling—it doesn't bother me, I don't want to seem disloyal, but it wasn't the big romance, you know. We just sort of drifted into it.
Martin I'm glad. (*Very seriously*) Because I have to tell you, I'm in love with you.
Cherry Oh, I am glad.
Martin And one further point—will you marry me?
Cherry Oh. That's sweet of you. (*She kisses him*)
Martin (*slightly puzzled*) It's not sweet of me, darling. I want an answer—yes or no?
Cherry (*genuinely surprised by his insistence*) Oh. (*Pause*) Well—since you insist, my darling—no.
Martin Would you care to rephrase that? Do you love me?
Cherry Of course I do.
Martin Well then, why don't you want to marry me?
Cherry (*putting a hand to his face*) Darling—marriage isn't ... I don't know how to put it ...
Martin Are you trying to tell me that marriage isn't the inevitable concomitant of love?
Cherry Probably. And however much I love you, and however much I want to be with you—and I do—I have no intention of becoming your —or anybody else's exclusive property.
Martin Hell, you really mean it—this women's lib bit, don't you?
Cherry Women's lib is a stereotyped and rather out-dated form of what I feel. But I do mean it.
Martin (*looking at her intently, genuinely shocked*) My God, you're a full time feminist.
Cherry Darling, tell me *one* thing. Why should we be married? We're

happy together. We can see each other whenever we like. We both have active and interesting careers—which are bound to clash.

Martin Why should my career clash with a company that markets some form of sporting equipment?

Cherry It's not as if I asked for the job, I inherited it from my husband.

Martin What happened to him then?

Cherry He died in Venezuela testing products for the firm . . .

Martin Oh, sorry.

Cherry I wouldn't be any good for you, darling—particularly if you became an M.P. That's what's so sad. You need a nice safe girl. You *need* marriage. I don't.

Martin (*after a long pause*) All right, then. Since you won't consider a freehold arrangement, what about a long lease? Come lib with me and be my love.

Cherry Darling, I thought you'd never ask. Even if it is a typically conditioned male reaction. Why don't you come and live with me? My flat's nearer the office, and then we'll choose a new one together.

Martin (*shaking his head doubtfully*) I don't know, Cherry. I may be old-fashioned but we lawyers . . .

Cherry You lawyers have fixed and totally honourable views on how two people should live together in sin. (*She puts her arms round him*) Poor darling, have I shocked you? Don't worry, you can pay the household bills if it will ease your conscience, and you can let your flat and we'll be rich.

Martin (*still doubtful*) It's a lovely idea, but I don't know what my firm will think—as for the constituents—

Cherry Perhaps it's time the constituents were educated to the realities of today.

Martin Hmmm—they might even come to respect an honest approach to the great social problems of the twentieth century—the unmarried working wife; the single parent family—the upright member with a social conscience . . .

Cherry Well you can make a political speech about it if you like but the argument is "your place or mine" and I have got a bigger bed.

Cherry walks into the kitchen

Martin True!

Martin follows Cherry off

The Lights fade, and come up on Cherry's office

Scene 5

Bill and Travers, the directors, enter the office

Travers Pull yourself together, Bill, and stop spluttering at me.

Bill Look here it's very bad form to make personal remarks about my d-disability.

Travers I said sputtering.
Bill Oh I thought you said—oh never mind. (*He flops into the chair*) I'm so tired.
Travers Do try and concentrate on business.
Bill It's difficult. Very difficult. I was on manoeuvres last night. You see I've met this fantastic girl . . .
Travers (*ignoring him*) Prince Ali Hassan has offered to put up the capital we require, and he's got absolutely flawless credentials.
Bill Well hardly flawless, I mean he's not British.
Travers But he's very rich.
Bill Travers, have you ever been in love?
Travers I've had my moments. Anyway the prince is head of an international conglomerate and he's prepared to do the deal immediately.
Bill (*dreamily*) —tall, slim, aristocratic . . .
Travers Yes, he is.
Bill Not him, Helen. (*He yawns*)
Travers (*taking no notice*) The prince wants to finalise the details over dinner tonight with Cherry. I must say, I don't see why he can't do it with me.
Bill Because she's prettier. (*Away in his dreams again*) Candlelight, Château Lafitte, crêpes Suzette . . .
Travers Very likely.
Bill That's what we had for dinner last night.
Travers (*in a military tone*) TAYLOR!
Bill Sir!
Travers That's better. (*Shaking his head*) Can't you ever forget the military syndrome?
Bill Why should I? I did very well in the Army, my C.O. wrote of me, "This officer never makes the same mistake twice".
Travers Probably made most of them once! Look—pay attention. (*Firmly*) Our problem is that Cherry's not keen on going out to dinner, says she's being used.
Bill Well we'll just have to persuade her, tell her it's for the good of the regiment and all that. By the way, what's he like, this prince chappie?
Travers Well he's got a lot of charm—about thirty thousand barrels a day actually. And he went to an English public school.
Bill Well that's different, which one?
Travers I think he was at Uppingham.

Travers exits

Bill Uppingham? Well I hope that's not how he spent his time! (*He starts to telephone. Humming to himself*) "Falling in love again, never wanted to—what am I to do? I can't h-h-h-h- . . ." Helen! This is . . . How did you know it was me?
Travers (*putting his head round the door*) TAYLOR!
Bill Good-bye, sir—coming darling . . .

Bill slams down the telephone and goes out after Travers
The Lights fade, then come up on Area 1

Act I, Scene 6   23

SCENE 6

The following evening

The Lights go up as Martin is letting himself into Cherry's flat, where he is now clearly established. He carries a large bunch of roses and a bottle of champagne. He is dressed in a black jacket and striped trousers

Martin (*calling as he closes the door*) Cherry! Anyone home?

The telephone rings, and he goes to answer it

(*On the telephone*) Hallo? . . . Ah, Lord Temple, good evening . . . Helen? Yes, well you know how it is—a sort of mutual antipathy overcame us—I suppose it all started because she just refused to accept my explanation of how I came to be in bed with another woman . . . Well, it's very good of you to say so, sir. I was rather hoping it wouldn't affect our business dealings but not every father would take that view . . . Oh, the constituency—you don't think they . . . They aren't? . . . They wouldn't? . . . They don't . . . I understand. Well, naturally I'm disappointed—but that's politics . . . You've *already* decided on another candidate—good, someone more experienced I suppose . . . More direct . . . *articulate* . . . BILL TAYLOR! B-BILL? I mean Bill? Yes, we have met. (*He rubs his jaw absently*) Anyway, it was kind of you to ring. I'll see you in Court. Good-bye. (*He hangs up*) Bill? My poor constituency. Oh, well. There will be martial law in Bromwich South!

He starts making preparations for a special evening with Cherry—collects a silver ice bucket from the kitchen, stands the champagne in it and places it on the coffee table in front of the sofa, then arranges the roses in a vase. He turns down the lights, turns up sweet music on the stereo. He walks about the room muttering, apparently rehearsing a proposal of marriage as he does these things

(*With gestures*) Cherry, we've been together for two months, nine beautiful weeks, and . . . No. (*He kneels by the sofa*) Darling, now that you know me better—would you consider abandoning your ludicrous affections of female emancipation . . . ? No. (*He gets up and becomes very business-like*) . . . Cherry, statistics have proved that *married* men suffer less from headaches and tension . . . (*He shakes his head*)

During the above, Cherry enters from the lift

Oh hell, darling—let's get married!

He hears the key in the lock and goes to meet Cherry, who rushes in, business-like, in a great hurry

Cherry Hallo, darling!

She gives Martin a quick routine kiss and bustles about, turning up the lights turning off the sweet music—totally unaware of the romantic ambiance created by Martin—oblivious of the champagne and roses

(*Still bustling about*) I am livid . . .
Martin Darling, I . . .
Cherry I am so angry you can't imagine. A real killer of a day—nothing went right—(*she turns on another light*)—quite chaotic—
Martin (*exasperated*) Will you stop buggering about with my ambiance and *listen*?
Cherry —and now I have to go out again to dinner. (*She moves towards the bathroom door*)
Martin Out? Oh, no! But I've made a whole lot of plans for this evening.

Cherry exits to the bathroom

Cherry (*off*) Oh, I'm sorry, darling. I'd much rather be with you, you know that—but this is a vital business thing—really vital.
Martin Business. Great. We've been together for two months, eight whole idyllic weeks. I plan a celebration, a little champagne, our favourite table at Nomico's, and you have a business engagement. Over dinner?

Sounds of Cherry in the bathroom. Martin continues shouting through the doorway

Cherry (*off*) I've told you, I wouldn't be doing it unless it was necessary. We've got this very important client—
Martin Don't tell me; you've got some Arab Sheikh who's made the most fantastic offer.
Cherry (*off*) —you see there's this Arab Sheikh who wants to buy a controlling interest in the firm. Actually he's more than a sheikh, he's a conglomerate—
Martin —and you need the capital to expand . . .
Cherry (*off*) He's made the most fantastic offer—and we really do need the capital to expand.
Martin God, it's like talking to yourself.
Cherry (*off*) Okay. He is, apparently, rather keen on me but I don't intend to let that make any difference.

Cherry emerges from the bathroom with a towel around her, cleaning her teeth. She takes her evening dress out of the cupboard

I promise you, I am only going to talk business. It's a purely public relations exercise.
Martin Exercise, no doubt. Relations—possibly; but I *hope* not public.
Cherry You needn't worry. I shall be home by eleven.
Martin All right, I forgive you. Do we have time for a kiss?

Cherry turns, her mouth full of foam and kisses him. He licks his lips as if tasting a rather bad sherry

Um. Colgate 'eighty-one. Now, what about a glass of champagne?
Cherry (*moving to the bathroom*) Darling, I can't *stand* champagne. Besides, I must keep a clear head, you know. Business.

Cherry exits

Martin (*muttering*) Funny business! (*He sits on the couch*) I wanted to re-open the subject of our marriage.

Cherry (*off*) Oh, not that again. I suspect you only want it for your career.

Martin (*quietly*) No, I want it for its own sake. If you're referring to my political career you're wrong anyway. That has drawn peacefully to a close.

Cherry enters and sits doing her make-up

Cherry Oh, darling, I'm sorry. What happened?

Martin They wanted someone more direct, more down-to-earth, more articulate. They wanted Bill.

Cherry (*laughing*) Bill—articulate. He's a one man silent majority! Oh— I'm sorry, darling.

Martin It doesn't matter. I'd been thinking—politics would have interfered too much in our married life anyway. Very intrusive, all those sittings, visits to the constituency. I don't need you for my career at all, don't you see? I just need you.

Cherry Oh, darling. I do understand really I do. But look, can we talk about it later? I'm really rather worried about this evening . . .

Martin How much do you know about this man?

Cherry Oh, quite a lot. He's a Prince—English public school, very good-looking . . .

Martin And *now* the good news?

Cherry (*sweetly*) That I shall know tonight.

Martin (*gloomily sipping his drink*) You'll forgive me for pointing out that you are, by agreeing to spend the evening with this man, simply being used by the male-orientated society you despise so much to achieve its morally dubious ends. (*He fixes himself another drink*)

Cherry (*worried, but determined that it will not shake the hand applying the eyeshadow*) That's a ridiculous overstatement—and rather an offensive one—there's nothing unusual about a senior partner negotiating a deal over dinner.

Martin Are you trying to tell me that if you were a fat, male, balding, senior partner commuting from Haywards Heath your prospective buyer would still be taking you to some questionable night spot? Now I come to think of it, I'm not quite sure what your Pleasure and Leisure company sells.

Cherry (*momentarily evasive*) Well, that's irrelevant . . . (*Suddenly angry*) Look, what I do to make my business a success is my own affair.

Martin Affair is what I'm afraid of . . .

Cherry I'm free to live my own life as best as I can and make my own mistakes in my own way. I don't come crying to you when things go wrong and I can do without your carping when they're going right!

Cherry exits to the bathroom

Martin (*shouting*) All right—go and discuss terms with your good-looking public school prospective buyer. And I hope he pays cash. Or perhaps he'd prefer it on whore-purchase!

Cherry returns, really angry, with a box of Kleenex

Cherry My God—you're not just a male chauvinist pig—you're a real, live, ordinary pig. Get your nasty little snout out of here. (*She throws the box of Kleenex at him*)

Martin (*retreating towards the sofa*) But we're equal. I can say what I like to you. Oblivious of your sex. And because of your liberated attitude you don't mind . . .

Cherry I bloody do mind! You're an insulting pig.

Martin I can even hit you if I like—(*he does so rather feebly*)—that's what equality of the sexes means.

She belts him back

Ouch!

They collapse on the sofa, shouting and grunting

Prince Hassan enters from the lift and rings Cherry's front doorbell. He is a romantic Arab dressed in flowing galabiyah and the headdress of a prince: a most civilized and sophisticated man, educated at Eton and Oxford: hugely wealthy and very amusing, with an eye for the ladies

Before the fight Cherry had been more or less ready to go out, but now her hair is a mess, clothing disarranged and make-up smudged

Cherry (*stopping in mid-blow*) Hell, he's here. The Prince.

Martin I didn't hear a camel draw up.

She gets up from the sofa

Cherry (*smoothing her dress*) My God, he mustn't find you here, it'll ruin everything.

Martin (*lying back on the sofa and grinning*) Oh, what a pity!

The Prince who has been ringing intermittently, stops ringing, looks at his watch, then starts knocking

There's someone at the door.

Cherry (*calling*) Who is it?

Prince It's me.

Martin I think it's him.

Prince Is there some password I need to get in here?

Martin Try abracadabra.

Cherry Ssh! (*Calling to the Prince*) Just coming! (*To Martin*) Oh, please darling—this is important. Hide—or go down the fire escape or something.

Martin We haven't got a fire escape.

Cherry Well. Please—stall him. Do something. (*She retreats towards the bathroom, still touching up her hair*)

Martin (*with heavy sarcasm*) What's in it for me?
Cherry I told you—*anything*.
Martin (*grabbing Cherry by the arm*) Right! I'll hold you to that. I'll draft a contract.
Cherry Just stall him!

Cherry exits into the bathroom

Martin (*to himself*) Stall him?

Martin puts on his jacket deep in thought and suddenly has an idea. Straightening his tie, etc., he stalks towards the flat door.

(*Opening the door*) Good evening, sir—did you ring?

Martin bows low as,—

the CURTAIN *falls*

ACT II

Scene 1

The same. A few seconds later

The Prince enters. He immediately assumes that Martin, in black coat and striped trousers, is the butler. He carries a bunch of roses and a bottle of champagne

Prince (*to Martin, in impeccable English*) Good evening. Would you be so kind as to tell your mistress that Prince Hassan Ali bin Ali Hassan al Shadeed is here?
Martin My—er-mistress. Certainly, sir. Will you take a seat? (*He goes to the bathroom door and knocks*) Madam . . . (*He turns to the Prince*) Er—what was the name again?
Prince Hassan Ali bin Ali Hassan.
Martin (*to himself*) Well, which?
Prince Just tell her Prince Hassan. Or Bertie, if you find it easier.
Martin Bertie? I think I prefer Prince Hassan, sir. (*Calling through the door*) Prince Hassan is here, Madam. (*Under his breath*) And wearing a very pretty frock, too.
Cherry (*off*) Hello, Bertie—make yourself at home. I shan't be a minute.
Prince (*calling*) I've brought a bottle of champagne. I hope you don't mind?
Cherry (*off*) Oh, how lovely, I *adore* champagne.

Martin reacts. Prince Hassan wanders round the sitting-room and notices the champagne in the ice bucket and roses in a vase on the coffee table

Prince How splendid! I see you have anticipated my thoughts. (*By a wave of his hand he indicates that Martin is to open the champagne*)
Martin I hope so sir. (*He unwraps and examines the Prince's bottle*) Ah! Dom Perignon. You'll—er—take the cold bottle first, sir. I'll just put this away for later. (*He whisks the Prince's champagne away to the kitchen and reappears with two glasses. As he opens the champagne*) I trust it's cold enough, sir? Not as well bred as the Dom Perignon but an honest little wine trying desperately to find its way in the world. It's from the south side of the slopes sir. (*Handing him a glass*) Muswell Hill.

During the above the Prince removes a cigarette from a gold cigarette case and holds it up for Martin to light. Martin looks blank then rushes for a lighter

(*With a nervous laugh as he holds the lighter*) Sorry for the delay, sir. I understood that gentlemen from your country didn't smoke?

Act II, Scene 1   29

The Prince takes a long swig of champagne before replying

(*Meaningfully*) Or drink.

The Prince exhales cigarette smoke into Martin's face with a charming smile

Prince Oh you know how it is, I once made a solemn vow to give up smoking and drinking.
Martin (*politely*) Of course, sir, and what about women?
Prince Oh and them too.
Martin And?
Prince It was the most boring twenty-four hours of my life.

Cherry enters from the bathroom, dressed for dinner and looking stunning

Cherry Bertie, good evening. Oh—you've got a drink— good.
Prince Er—yes. Your man has been looking after me exceedingly well.
Cherry (*with a nervous glance at Martin*) Oh, my man—yes. Good.

Martin hands Cherry a glass of champagne on a salver

Martin (*deferentially*) Er—you'll join His Highness in a glass of champagne —madam? (*Under his breath*) I know how you appreciate it.
Cherry (*turning to the Prince*) So sweet of you to bring it, Bertie.
Prince Not at all.
Martin (*under his breath to Cherry*) Don't go overboard. This is Marks and Sparks. We'll 'ave the good stuff later.
Cherry (*taking the glass from the salver*) Thank you—er—Briggs.

Martin glares at her

Prince How beautiful you look.

Martin stands back and admires her too, beaming approvingly. He practically says, "Charming, charming"

And how lucky I am that you are dining with me tonight.
Cherry (*with a girlish laugh*) You look pretty—er—chic yourself.
Martin (*wincing at the pun*) Oh, madam!

Cherry indicates the sofa. She and the Prince sit. Martin fusses around arranging cushions, bringing an ashtray for the Prince, determined not to miss anything

Prince (*looks down at his dishdasha*) Oh, I apologize for this. I have come straight from the National Day Celebrations at our Embassy.
Cherry How colourful!
Prince Bloody boring actually. No booze, you know. I see no hope for the Arab nations until they legalize alcoholic stimulants ... (*He swigs champagne*)

Martin nods sympathetically and then offers to refill his glass

Martin More champagne, sir? Or would you prefer to change to Ribena?
Prince (*holding out his glass. To Cherry*) I hope you won't feel too con-

spicuous being seen with me in this gear? Bloody wogs—taking over the whole of London, you know.

Martin raises his eyebrows as if to say, "Is that right?" The Prince taps the ash off his cigarette. Martin leaps to place an ashtray at the last minute. The Prince misses and flicks ash on Cherry

Cherry (*slightly annoyed*) Oh, really Briggs—that was very clumsy.
Martin Beg pardon, madam. His Highness's intentions eluded me at the last . . .
Prince (*conversationally, to Cherry*) In my country we cut off the hand of a clumsy servant.

Martin, behind the sofa, "shoots" his coat-cuff, concealing his hand and makes a threatening gesture at the Prince

Martin (*in clipped tones*) With respect, sir—I fail to see—what that would do—to improve his dexterity.
Cherry Thank you, Briggs, that will be all.

Martin goes towards the kitchen door

Prince Oh—(*turning to his bouquet on the floor by the sofa*)—I've brought you some roses.
Cherry (*taking them, delighted*) Oh, how sweet of you! Aren't they lovely? Thank you.

Martin, hovering near the kitchen door, pointedly moves the vase containing his roses to a table nearer Cherry. Cherry looks around helplessly

Cherry Er—Briggs?
Martin Madam?
Cherry Would you put these in water for me?
Martin (*snatches them, with a black look at the Prince*) Certainly Madam. (*He walks majestically towards the kitchen door*) What poor little things! I shall try and find them an oasis.

Martin exits to the kitchen

Prince (*in a stage whisper*) He seems very liberated, your manservant.
Cherry But one has to allow them a certain amount of latitude nowadays, you know; otherwise they all go and work for Arabs. Oops, sorry!
Prince What a terrible fate! If we become partners you must visit me some day. I have a summer house by the sea, the sand is dead white, and the sea dark blue, great grey dolphins play about my yacht which lies at anchor off the palm fringed shore—I will send my private jet for you . . .

Martin's head appears round the kitchen door with an aggrieved look: then he returns from the kitchen bearing the Prince's roses which he has placed unceremoniously in a chamber pot. He places it on the coffee-table near the sofa, pushes one or two roses into place and stands back to admire his handiwork

Act II, Scene 1

(*Looking at the pot*) An interesting receptacle.
Martin (*loftily*) An early example of primitive English your Highness.
Prince Thank you, Briggs. I know a po when I see one. (*To Cherry*) Now my dear I've booked a table at Nomico's—I hope you like it.
Cherry *Absolutely* my favourite restaurant.

Martin, with an aggrieved look, moves behind the couch and eyes the Prince suspiciously

Prince And then I thought we might go to Annabel's.
Cherry Oh. I can't say I really like nightclubs.

Martin smiles approvingly

Prince Oh, what a shame. I've just bought it.

Martin puts his tongue out behind the Prince's back

Cherry And of course they're hardly the best places to discuss business.
Prince (*looking at her longingly*) Of course. Business before pleasure. But I shall be very disappointed if we have not disposed of our business by the end of the first course or at least the second course.
Martin (*hissing into Cherry's ear*) Watch out for the assault-course—more champagne, your Highness? (*He offers the bottle*)
Prince No thank you. (*To Cherry*) Are you ready my dear. Perhaps we should go?
Cherry Of course, I'll get my coat. Why don't you get the lift, Bertie?

She goes towards the built-in cupboard. The Prince goes towards the front door, collecting his coat and cane from Martin, then goes to the corridor. Martin bows him out. Cherry moves in with her coat. Martin moves to help her into it

Martin The magic carpet's out of order, sir. Allow me, madam.
Cherry Thank you, Briggs. And Briggs . . .
Martin Madam?
Cherry (*icily*) Your behaviour was quite appalling. You're fired.
Martin Well, I'm sorry, madam, but I haven't been a butler very long. Besides, you can't fire me, I live here.
Cherry We'll see about that. You did your very best to make fools out of Bertie and me.
Martin No, madam; there, I think, the Almighty and Allah forestalled me.
Cherry Very funny. (*She moves towards the door*) You must realize, Briggs, dear, that this evening is only part of a commercial operation.
Martin Of course, madam, darling. Purely business.
Cherry I shan't be late. Will you wait up for me, Briggs?
Martin Er—I may ring up a business acquaintance of mine—and take her to a night club.
Cherry You're a bastard, Briggs.
Martin Quite so, madam.

Cherry goes to the corridor. Martin follows her out. The Prince is standing by the open lift door and Martin bows low as they enter the lift

Good night, madam—your Highness.

Cherry and the Prince exit

Martin bows towards the lift

Helen opens her door and regards Martin's rear as he bows

Helen Mecca's the other way.
Martin The city, maybe. I think they're going to the ballroom.
Helen Looks like an Arab take-over. Have you lost her already?
Martin Certainly not, it's just a commercial operation.
Helen (*raising a languid eyebrow and shrugging her shoulders*) Poor girl, times are hard, I suppose.
Martin Not *that* kind of commercial operation. It's a massive Arab conglomerate that wants to take her over.
Helen Well, I've heard of gang-bangs, but that's ridiculous.
Martin Look, why not come in for a drink? He left behind some marvellous champagne.
Helen (*moving lazily into Cherry's flat*) Thought you'd never ask.

Martin follows her into the flat

I'm sorry about the constituency, Daddy told me. (*She sits on the couch*)
Martin (*smiling*) Daddy told me too, after you'd told Daddy. (*He moves to the kitchen door and returns with a bottle of champagne and two glasses*) No loss, really. I don't think the constituency and I really deserved each other. I'm not sure they deserved Bill either. How do you think he'll get on. (*He opens the champagne*)
Helen All right, I think, in a military sort of way.
Martin Military?
Helen Yes, didn't you know? That's why Daddy chose him as the candidate. Daddy can't resist the solid military virtues, guts, loyalty, obedience, leadership . . .
Martin He couldn't lead *me* down a fire-escape.
Helen They say his men would follow him anywhere.
Martin Out of curiosity, I suppose.
Helen He's full of aggressive spirit, you must admit.
Martin (*rubbing his jaw*) You can say that again.
Helen (*deadpan*) He's full of the aggressive spirit, you must admit.

The telephone rings. Martin toasts Helen silently and lifts the receiver

Martin (*on the telephone*) Hello . . . That was quick, where are you? . . . Ah! Yes, the Rolls . . . I suppose the Prince is on the other line? . . . of course, he's watching T.V. . . . What folder? . . . (*Indignantly*) Bring it to Nomico's? I certainly will not . . . No. You've got a nerve asking . . . Well he can't hear what I'm saying—(*gleefully*)—and as you can't answer back I'm taking this opportunity of explaining some hard facts

Act II, Scene 1

... I'm sick of your bloody-mindedness under the guise of female independence or so-called business opportunity, and I'm beginning to hold out very little hope for a successful outcome to this relationship, unless you change your attitude—and don't hang up or I shall discontinue this conversation immediately. (*He looks at Helen and shrugs*) You've got to make up your mind whether you want to be a woman or a businessman.

Helen pours him some champagne

(*To Helen*) Thank you, darling. Don't spill it. (*Into the telephone*) I said thank you, darling, don't spill it ... Champagne. It's this woman, you see. She keeps topping up my glass. And you can stuff the folder! (*He hangs up, smiles at Helen and drinks*)

Helen You weren't very nice to her.

Martin I know, but stern measures were required. She's been mucking me about for too long. The velvet glove has failed. We must try the mailed fist.

Helen (*a little drunk*) Bill's always mailing his fist; special delivery. (*She throws a punch*) Bonk!

Martin So I remember.

Helen (*with a little giggle*) He's awfully strong, isn't he?

Martin Did he try and strong arm the selection committee?

Helen Oh, yes. (*She imitates Bill*) "Now pay attention! I'm not going to say this twice!" Trouble is, poor dear can hardly say it once!

Martin (*raising his glass*) Anyway, here's to him. You and the Incredible Hulk.

Helen (*raising her glass*) You and Bionic Woman.

Bill appears, getting out of the lift, approaches the front door and presses the bell

Martin and Helen freeze guiltily

Martin (*calling*) Who is it?
Bill Bill T-T-Taylor.

Martin closes his eyes for a moment in horror, while instinctively rubbing his jaw

Helen discards her languid, rather drunken dignity, jumps over the couch and hides in the bathroom

Martin opens his eyes—Helen has vanished. Bill presses the bell again. Martin shrugs and goes to the door

Martin That was quick! Coming. (*He opens the door and stands quickly back*)

Bill enters and glares at Martin suspiciously. Martin smiles in what he hopes is a disarming manner

What can I do for you?

Bill Cherry sent me to f-f-f- . . .
Martin (*anxiously*) Fight?
Bill (*shaking his head*) F-f-f- . . .
Martin Give me a clue. Four letters, I expect . . .
Bill *Fetch the folder!*
Martin Of course—carry on.

Bill looks suspiciously round the room

Bill It's not here. I'll look in the off-off-off- . . .
Martin Off you go then. (*He points to the office door*)

Helen crawls a little out of the bathroom

Bill Office!

Bill moves to the office door. Helen crawls further out. As Bill goes into the office—Area 3—she gets to her feet and weaves her way to the door. There is a noise as Bill opens the desk, extracts the file and Helen leaps out of the front door and slams it. Bill shoots back into the flat

W-what was that?
Martin (*innocently*) What was what? (*He retreats upstage*)
Bill (*striding across to the door and opening it*) Never mind. G-g-goodnight.

Helen, who has just managed to open her own door, now pretends she is coming out

Helen (*with deadly drunken emphasis*) What are you doing coming out of that woman's flat?
Bill Helen! But I w-w-wasn't . . .
Helen (*coldly*) You clearly was! Looks pretty fishy to me. (*She stands aside and points into her flat*) I think you owe me an explanation!

Bill nods meekly and exits into Helen's flat. Helen turns and winks at Martin who has put his head out as—Bill comes rushing back out and bumps into Helen. Martin closes the door and begins to clear up the mess. The Lights fade on the lounge. Meanwhile Bill makes for the lift

Bill Oh, no, Helen, I can't stay now. I've got to deliver . . .
Helen That can wait Billy, haven't you forgotten that you're addressing the Conservative Mothers Union tomorrow?
Bill Oh, Lord, yes, so I am. Well look I've made some notes—would you hear me Helen, give me the benefit of your—would you please, please! (*He hands her the file and takes notes from his pocket*)
Helen I think I'd better. Last time you told the Boiler Makers Union they couldn't get a rise if they downed tools . . .
Bill A slip of the tongue. There was no reason for them to throw their sandwiches at me when I left. I was covered in s-s-sandwiches. This time I thought I'd start with something really definite.
Helen Oh good.
Bill I am your candidate. I fit the BILL, I am TAYLOR made for the job, My n-n-n-name is Bill Taylor.

Act II, Scene 2   35

Helen (*drily*) That ought to grab them.
Bill Yes. Then I thought I'd go on, "Most mothers are women. My mother was a woman and I am very conscious of the problems of the Conservative mother in Labour—(*he turns over the sheet*)—ah—in Labour constituencies. HA—HA . . ." Then I develop that a bit, emphasizing the difficulties and how the Conservative government will create jobs for the many thousands who are out of work.
Helen Millions!
Bill Are there really? No one ever tells me anything! Okay. "The Conservative government will provide jobs for the many thousands—and millions who are out of work—provided of course they vote Conservative . . . And then I thought I'd finish off . . . (*He goes to the lift*)
Helen Oh, yes do, for God's sake!
Bill I thought I'd finish up "Good-bye and good luck—and now are there any questions?"

The lift doors close in Bill's face, trapping his notes in the door. The notes travel down the lift doors and disappear at the bottom

Helen Yes, may we have another candidate.

Helen looks at the file Bill has forgotten and exits into her flat

The Lights fade on the corridor and come up on Area 1

SCENE 2

About three hours later

Martin enters from the kitchen, brandy in one hand—fat cigar in the other—he is obviously a little drunk. Travers enters the office (Area 3) and switches on the light. He has on an overcoat and bowler hat. He goes to Cherry's desk, opens the drawer, looks for the all-important folder, fails to find it and shuts the drawer in exasperation. He looks at his watch, yawns and settles down in a chair, immediately falls asleep and starts to snore. The noise is heard through the door and Martin puzzled, goes across and listens. Suspecting a burglar, he flexes his muscles, throws open the door and jumps in, Karate-fashion

Martin Hah! . . . Oh, sorry.
Travers (*waking with a start*) What? Who are you?
Martin Oh, it's you, Mr Travers. Sorry I thought it was a burglar. Oh, I'm Martin Barclay, we've met with Cherry.
Travers Have we? (*He peers at him*) So we have.
Martin Working late, aren't you? It's nearly midnight.
Travers (*yawning*) I know, long past my bedtime but Miss Winters rang and asked me to be here when she came back from her dinner engagement in case she wanted to talk business with the Prince, I think but was afraid he might, er, take advantage of the, er, circumstances—seize the . . . She wanted someone here who could—redress the balance.

(*Vaguely*) She wanted a rather urgent folder we put together for her, too, but I can't find it.

Martin I think Bill's taken it. Look, why don't you come next door and have a drink while you're waiting. We can hear when they come into the office.

Travers Ooh, thank you, that would be much more comfortable.

They go into the flat

Martin I've had a perfectly awful evening, you know. I had to pretend I was the butler.

Travers Really? I've never heard of that one before. French maids used to be popular—and slaves—but it's all part of the servant-master syndrome, I suppose. Butler, indeed!

Martin No, you don't understand, Mr Travers. Cherry was trying to impress the Prince—and—er—oh never mind, would you like a whisky?

Travers Thank you, Mr Barclay.

Martin Oh, please call me Martin.

Travers How do you do—my name's Cedric.

Martin I am sorry. Do you mind if I still call you Mister Travers?

Travers I prefer it, actually.

Martin Whisky?

Travers Thank you.

Martin (*reaching out and taking hold of the coat*) Do take this off, Mr Travers.

The bowler and overcoat come off and Mr Travers has on his pyjama top underneath

Travers (*struggling*) I was in a hurry. (*He takes his drink and sits down. He starts to nod off again*)

Martin How is the business going?

Travers Huh? Oh, fine.

Martin (*sitting; conversationally*) I've never really known what part of the leisure industry you are in. Cherry never talks much about it. All I know is she wants to inject more capital so you can expand.

Travers Expand yes—we're trying to reach a wider public, embrace all ages.

Martin You mean youth groups, old people's organizations, that sort of thing?

Travers Excellent idea, I'll remember that.

Martin And I presume that is what the Prince is for, eh?

Travers Prince—yes—Pleasure and Leisure. (*He snores*)

Martin (*smiles*) I know what you mean. (*He sips his drink*)

We hear noises, and Cherry enters her office from the outer door

She switches off the light and opens the flat door and comes face to face with Martin. She glares at him and slams the door. This wakes up Travers

Travers Ah! Hallo ...

Cherry (*to Travers*) Where were you? I could have been half-way to the mysterious East by now for all your help. (*She pours herself a drink*)
Travers I was standing by in a thoroughly alert position—but unfortunately Nemesis suddenly overcame me.
Cherry Anyway, he's agreed to the deal and the contract is going to be ready for signature at eleven in the morning. Make sure Jenkins, our solicitor, is there. (*She fixes a drink and sits*)
Travers Of course, and congratulations.
Cherry Thank you. (*To Martin, angrily*) You see what a woman can do—single-handed.
Martin (*to Travers*) Has it ever occurred to you, Mr Travers, how indefatigably women go on about being women? On and on?
Travers Oh, yes, often.
Martin Half the population of the world is female, so it is not that remarkable . . .
Travers Remarkable . . .
Martin And yet, judging by the media, women seem to be in a perpetual state of surprise over the fact.
Travers Surprise . . .
Cherry Do stop being so boring.
Martin *Me*, boring? Every day we have to read more yawn-making articles about the libido; how to get your man; how to keep your man; how to get rid of him; personal hygiene; the problem of unwanted hair . . .
Travers (*touching his head*) I haven't got any unwanted hair.
Martin Now men don't go on like that about being men. Do you?
Travers Well—er—I . . .
Martin You'd go a long way before you found a publication which depends for its circulation on articles about shaving, double hernia or athlete's foot.
Travers That's true.
Cherry The usual male chauvinist rubbish. It's still a man's world.
Martin (*glaring at her*) Three-quarters of the wealth of the United States is in the hands of women—their husbands having collapsed on the treadmill of corporation life and retired to an early grave. In certain areas of Botswana the available males parade—like pedigree bulls to be selected by predatory females and led off to a life of reproductive frenzy; and in England, who is the most powerful and dominating executive in the civilized world . . . ?
Travers The Queen! Such a nice lady. (*He begins to nod off*)
Martin (*shouting across a recumbent Travers at Cherry*) The entire thrust of the advertising world is directed at *women*. I know of women who are totally unaware of the existence of men except as plumbers, gardeners and providers of little envelopes stuffed with money on Friday nights.
Cherry (*shouting back*) I'm the one who stuffs the envelopes on Friday nights!
Martin (*shouting*) Stop shouting! You're embarrassing Cedric.
Cherry (*loudly*) SORRY! (*To Travers, quietly*) Sorry. (*To Martin*) My fault.

Martin Yes.
Cherry Yes, what?
Martin Yes, *sir!*
Travers (*struggling up*) Well, I think it's time for my shut-eye. Sorry about the folder, Cherry. I couldn't find it. (*He puts on his coat*)
Martin Ah yes, the one that Briggs was so stupid about.
Cherry Yes, the one I've been trying to get hold of all evening.
Martin Well I think you'll find that Bill has it—next door.
Cherry Well I shall need it for our discussion with the Prince's legal people in the morning. Could you get it for me?
Martin I'd rather not, if you don't mind. I'm not one of your employees and I don't particularly want any part of your rather dubious negotiations.
Travers Er—it is a little late now, Cherry. Let me pick it up in the morning. I'll make sure you have it on your desk by nine. Good night.

Travers lets himself out and goes out through the office

They hardly notice his departure

Cherry (*furiously*) My God, you pompous ass! That's twice you could have helped me out this evening when I really needed you. But you're too damned self-important to lift a finger.
Martin On the contrary—I struggled to maintain the ludicrous fiction of being your manservant—while that refugee from the *Desert Song* oiled his way all over you.
Cherry And another thing—who was that woman you had here when I rang you up?
Martin Somebody who showed a little more sympathy and understanding than you ever will over the position you have put me in. It's no good. We can't go on like this. Cherry, I've had enough.
Cherry All right. If your precious image is liable to get tarnished, then you'd better move out of this flat!
Martin Thank you. I've already arranged to move out. This is impossible. (*He picks up his jacket and goes to the door*) Cherry, I loved you and I have repeatedly offered you the highest honour a man can bestow—my hand in marriage. And what do I get in return? A sort of all night French farce in fancy dress! Well, it may hold all kinds of Eastern promise for you but not for me. It's quite clear that you are totally indifferent to my feelings . . . So you can keep your independence—and I will keep mine. Good night Ms Chairperson! . . .

The Lights fade, then come up on Area 3

Scene 3

The next morning

The telephone rings in the office. The door opens and Mr Travers enters, awake and alert for a change, carrying a file of documents. He answers the telephone

Act II, Scene 3

Travers Hello—Travers here . . . Ah! Mr Barclay, what can I do for you? I'm afraid Cherry is tied up and we have a crisis on our hands . . . Yes, the Prince is due any moment and our solicitor is nowhere to be found . . . Oh, I am sorry . . . Then you did have a bust up. I thought when I left it was blowing up for wind . . . Dorothy and I don't have many storms, the odd shower as it were, when Willis widdles on the carpet . . . I'll tell Cherry you rang . . . Good-bye. (*He hangs up*)

He has no sooner put the telephone down when it rings again

(*On the telephone*) Hello? . . . Ah! Jenkins, Jenkins and Potter . . . Any sign of young Mr Jenkins? . . . Oh dear, his grandmother's funeral . . . I am sorry. What about old Mr Jenkins? . . . Of course same funeral . . . What about old Mr Potter? . . . Oh dear, I am sorry . . . Passed away last month. Well please try and get me someone, preferably someone who'll last until lunchtime! . . . It's very urgent . . . Good-bye.

Cherry enters

Cherry Have you got hold of any of our solicitors yet?
Travers No they seem to be a dying breed, Jenkins, Jenkins and Potter are practically extinct.
Cherry We must just stall and wait for a miracle.
Travers I've 'phoned Poulson and Wells, they may be able to send somebody round in a couple of hours.
Cherry Oh Lord!
Travers (*patting her shoulder*) Don't worry. We'll sort it out somehow. I'm sure the Prince will wait a day or two.
Cherry It's not just the business—*everything* seems to be going wrong.
Travers Martin?

She nods

Yes, I'm so sorry. He rang to say he was coming round—
Cherry (*looks up hopefully*) This morning? Oh, when?
Travers —to collect his things.
Cherry (*shaking her head*) It's my fault. I've seen it coming. But it is difficult to change, Cedric.
Travers (*gently*) *I* know. Don't worry.
Cherry Perhaps when we've done this deal . . .
Travers Don't leave it too late, Cherry.

There is a knock on the door and the Prince enters, this time immaculately dressed in a Savile Row suit. He swoops elegantly on Cherry's hand and kisses it gallantly

Prince Good morning, my dear. You look charming—(*hastily*)—and business-like, of course. The sooner we get the business side over, the sooner I can take my new partner to lunch. Here you are. (*He opens his briefcase and takes out three copies of a contract, several pages thick. He hands them to Cherry and Travers*)
Cherry Thank you.

Prince Mr Travers.

Travers (*beginning to flick over the pages*) I'll start reading. I hope this has a happy ending—we are of course waiting for our legal adviser who is on his way.

Cherry leans over Travers' shoulder as they study the documents

Martin comes out of the lift, listens at the door for a moment, then lets himself into the flat. He goes to the cupboard and takes out a suitcase, puts it on the sofa and starts to pack, bringing things from the bedroom

The Lights come up on Area 1

Cherry It's obviously a weighty document. We shall have to study it carefully.

Prince Of course. But don't take too long. I have booked our table for lunch in exactly one hour as I am flying to New York this afternoon.

Travers You couldn't take a later plane?

Prince It would be the same plane, Mr Travers—my own Tri-Star—whenever I took it, but I cannot delay its departure as my appointment in New York is not negotiable. I am quite prepared to settle our deal now but I will not be back for at least a month and if it is not finalized, who knows—other pressures may change my mind.

He smiles, but they get the message

Cherry Do sit down, Bertie—and excuse me for just one moment.

The Prince and Travers sit and Cherry goes into the flat and goes to the telephone. She sees Martin and checks momentarily

(*Coldly*) Good morning.

Martin Morning. I didn't expect you to be here. I've just—come to collect my things.

Cherry So I see. And I've come to telephone.

Martin (*deliberately offhand*) Oh, please carry on—don't mind me.

Cherry (*dialling*) There are some things of yours in the fridge, too. Half a bottle of Beaujolais and some rather smelly cheese. Perhaps you'd remove them as well. (*Into the telephone*) Poulson and Wells? . . . Oh hello, this is Miss Winters of P & L. Have you any news of a lawyer for us? . . . No . . . I see . . . Thank you . . . Good-bye. (*She hangs up*)

Martin Cherry, I . . .

Cherry Yes?

Martin Last night—er—perhaps I was a bit—precipitate—I'd had a few drinks.

Cherry You were drunk. You'd drunk most of the Prince's bottle of Dom Perignon—and heaven knows what else . . .

Martin That is a ridiculous and unfair exaggeration. I was not drunk.

Cherry Drunk and jealous.

Martin I was neither—although I had every right to be both. The spectacle of your prostituting yourself in the name of good business was distasteful in the extreme.

Act II, Scene 3   41

Cherry Well I haven't got time to argue.

Martin continues to pack. He begins to fold a shirt carefully, then screws it into a ball and throws it in the suitcase. Cherry continues in a more conciliatory tone of voice

The fact is—I'm in a bit of a fix. Do you know of a good lawyer?
Martin Are you deliberately trying to be insulting?
Cherry No, I'm sorry. Let me put it another way. (*In a rush*) Will you be my instant legal representative—here and now?
Martin (*flippantly, still packing*) Certainly—what charge are you on?
Cherry I've got this man in there who wants to buy a controlling interest in the Company—
Martin (*with a slight sneer*) Just a man—or a Prince?
Cherry He's a conglomerate, actually.
Martin And the controlling interest is in you, not the Company?
Cherry Oh, come on! This is business, Martin. I need a lawyer now. Will you do it?
Martin (*after a pause*) Strictly business?
Cherry Strictly business.
Martin Give me the contract.

Cherry gives him the contract. He flicks through the pages professionally

Martin Stall for a few minutes and I'll call you when I'm ready.
Cherry Thank you. (*She turns towards the office door*)
Martin There's one problem . . .
Cherry (*stops at door*) What?
Martin (*looking up from the papers*) I doubt if your Prince will be very impressed by the legal opinion and negotiating powers of your butler.
Cherry Oh Lord! I'd forgotten. (*She moves towards the office door*) You work on the contract, I'll think of something.

Cherry goes into the office before Martin can reply. He shrugs and studies the papers. The Prince rises as Cherry enters the office

Gentlemen, our legal adviser has arrived. He's in the flat and just checking a few points. (*She takes a box file out of a drawer and hands it to Travers*) Would you take this into him, please?
Travers (*in a whisper to Cherry*) But this is full of—er—you know . . .
Cherry Yes. (*Sweetly*) I *know* what it is. Mr Barclay will be needing it.
Travers (*trying to follow*) Will he? Ah, yes—of course, Mister Barclay? Oh—excuse me, Your Highness. (*He rises and as he goes into the flat he shoots a confused look at Cherry. As he shuts the door he looks equally puzzled at Martin*) Good morning, Mr Barclay. Cherry has sent me in with these. (*He opens the box file and offers it to Martin*)
Martin (*glancing inside*) Morning, Mr Travers, what have we got here? Disguises! Oh—good thinking. How on earth did you get them so quickly?
Travers We keep them in stock. Some people need them for their fantasies.
Martin (*still reading the papers*) Fantasies?

Travers Er—why do you need disguising?
Martin I told you—when I met the Prince last night—I was the butler.

Martin exits into the bathroom

Travers (*confused but resilient*) Ah! Of course I remember—so confusing.

As Martin exits to the bathroom Travers sits on the couch and engrosses himself in the contract. Meanwhile Cherry and the Prince quietly discuss business and Cherry shows him the folder

Prince (*smiling*) So finally we see the contents of the elusive folder. Interesting. (*He reads*)

The office telephone rings. Cherry answers

Cherry Hallo? . . . Yes, Bill . . . You wish to resign? Have you been elected already? . . . Oh, from the firm . . . I think you're right. You should. I agree . . . No, I shouldn't reconsider . . . No, don't . . . Good-bye.
Prince Someone resigned?
Cherry Yes, while we are waiting. Mr Travers was very anxious to show you some of our latest products. Perhaps I could . . .
Prince There's really no need, my dear. I don't share his enthusiasm. I prefer to get my kicks from the profit column of the balance sheet—unless of course you are going to give me a personal demonstration?
Cherry Not exactly. This is Monique. (*She points to the folder*) Mr Travers is particularly fond of her, she's our new inflatable lady.
Prince Well, if that's what turns him on. I sometimes think I'll never understand the English. A perfectly respectable businessman with a rubber woman. . . .

Martin enters from the bathroom in wig and moustache

Travers Oh—very—commanding.
Martin I can't say I'd trust a lawyer who looked like this.
Travers Try these. (*He hands a pair of sun glasses over*) And just a hint of the—aggressive.
Martin (*putting them on*) Mr Travers, I only want to be normal. (*Trying his own glasses*) How's this?
Travers Excellent!
Martin Well here goes. You'd better ask His Highness to step this way.
Travers Good luck. (*He goes into the office*) Mr Barclay is ready now your Highness.

Travers opens the door and they go in. Cherry double-takes on Martin and stifles a laugh

Cherry (*introducing*) Bertie, this is Mr Barclay.
Martin (*bowing*) Salaams, your Highness.
Prince *Wa-alaikum as-salaam ya akhee. Kayf haalak? Kayf as saha?*
Martin (*nonplussed*) Ah very likely . . .
Prince I do speak a little schoolboy English, you know.

Martin I know you do—I mean—you do? Well, sir, shall we start?
Prince Most certainly. (*Peering at Martin*) Haven't we met somewhere? There's something about you that's familiar. Do you do business in the Middle East?
Martin Mostly the Far East, sir. Now shall we get down to business? May I first draw your attention to paragraph five in the contract—clause four. I think we should clarify exactly what is meant by these figures—
Travers (*to Cherry*) That would be nice.
Martin —during last years trading, Pleasure and Leisure turnover increased by twenty-three per cent, while profits before tax rose by no less than thirty-nine point four per cent to *two hundred and thirty-four thousand pounds*—(*he reads in wonder*)—during a period in which a mild recession in the Malaysian rubber market had an adverse effect on sales —(*he looks up from the paper and explains to the Prince*)—that would, of course, affect many of the company's products—

Martin turned to Cherry and Travers as if for confirmation. They nod. He improvizes

—er, hockey-stick handles, wicket-keeping gloves, body armour and so on . . .

Travers shakes his head. Cherry nods

Prince (*puzzled*) Wicket-keeping gloves? Body armour?
Martin An old English pastime, your Highness—to protect the more vulnerable parts of the anatomy from fast . . .
Prince Balls.
Martin I beg your pardon, sir?
Prince Sounds more like cricket to me.
Martin Exactly sir. (*He shrugs and goes back to the contract*) The current years trading figures appear to be even more promising and I think you can be satisfied—
Prince Ah! (*Still trying to place him*) Are you a member of Boodles?
Martin (*shaking his head*) The Garrick—satisfied that you are becoming associated with a highly successful trading organization with unique opportunities for expansion. I think, therefore, that it is slightly presumptuous of you to expect to obtain fifty-one per cent of the equity for the figure you are offering.
Prince Do you?
Martin Are you not legally represented, sir?
Prince I have a degree in law.
Martin I see. Well, a cash sum of two hundred thousand pounds when last year's balance sheet showed . . .
Prince Just a minute. What do you suggest, Mr—er—Barclay?
Martin I think it would be reasonable for us to insist on safeguarding our present directors' interests by an *ex gratia* payment of twenty-five thousand pounds each?

Martin looks enquiringly at the Prince, who nods

Prince That would seem to be entirely reasonable.
Martin Oh, good. And now, perhaps we could examine Clause five-A.
Prince My solicitor, who drafted the contract, inserted this clause to cover the possibility of reduced profit margins as a result of probable tax increases in the next Budget . . .
Martin Not at all. That eventuality is taken care of in Clause eighteen-B. In any case, you can't expect to legislate for every eventuality. My client and you will be in this together.
Prince (*after a long pause*) I accept your terms. Have the amendments typed immediately and I will sign them—on one condition, that you, sir, are made Chairman of the Board.
Martin (*looking amazed*) That's very good of you, sir, but I'm afraid I'm already fully employed.
Prince Oh, but I insist! As I see it—and I *am* buying a controlling interest, I believe? The present directors will do all the day-to-day work and you as the Chairman will only be responsible for major policy decisions and overall co-ordination. As to salary—how would twenty thousand a year suit you?

Martin sits in amazed silence

(*Taking Martin's silence as refusal*) Twenty-five?
Martin Really, sir, I am most honoured—but I couldn't really consider . . .
Prince Thirty?
Martin No, I really couldn't—(*pause*)—pounds or dollars?
Prince Pounds, of course—(*with a charming smile*)—though if you prevaricate much longer, dollars may be more advantageous.
Martin I accept—on condition that I need only attend six meetings a year.
Prince Done. (*He holds out his hand*)
Travers (*to Cherry, under his breath*) I rather think he *has* been . . .
Prince Will you kindly have that drawn into the contract and I will sign it after lunch . . . it will, of course, require all your signatures as well. Thank you, gentlemen. Come, Cherry, the goat, as we say in my country, is on the table. (*He beckons Cherry towards the door*)
Martin (*in a murmur*) And the lamb to the slaughter.

The Prince reaches the door and turns. Martin bows

Prince I've got it. Lord Carbridges clean-up-Soho campaign—you were prosecuting council!
Martin Er—that's right.
Prince I didn't recognize you—but, then, of course, you were wearing your wig.

The Prince goes to the corridor followed by Cherry, who turns acidly to Martin

Cherry Thank you Mr Barclay for looking after our interests so capably. (*Under her breath*) And as one prostitute to another—welcome to the trade.

The Prince and Cherry exit into the lift

Act II, Scene 3 45

Martin (*relaxing*) Phew!
Travers Congratulations. Masterly, if I may say so, quite masterly.
Martin Thank you Mr Travers. An element of bluff and I hope the contract *is* okay. I'll read it now—before the signatures.
Travers (*smiling*) An ex-gratia payment of twenty-five thousand pounds—*very* nice. I think I will purchase a convertible Ferrari, with all the extras . . .
Martin (*surprised*) What colour do you fancy?
Travers Blonde, I think.
Martin (*casually, while reading*) By the way, now that I'm Chairman, what exactly do we sell?
Travers Oh, don't you know? Well, I hope you'll be pleasantly surprised . . . (*He hands Martin a glossy P.A.L. brochure*) This is Pleasure and Leisure —PAL for short.
Martin (*turning the pages, as revelation dawns*) My God, a sex shop! And I thought you sold sporting equipment!
Travers Well, you could call it that. It's not just one sex shop, you know. (*With missionary zeal*) It's a whole chain.
Martin A whole chain!
Travers Nationwide—linking the libidos of those countless, frightened, thousands who stifle their natural longings, guilt-ridden at the suppression of natural desires—yearning for the reality of a perfectly normal sexual fantasy . . .
Martin You amaze me.
Travers And so I should. Then they come to us. (*His eyes shine with crusading fervour*) Eureka! We show them the way to a new life—a life of fulfilment and normality.
Martin (*looking down at the brochure*) That doesn't look very normal.
Travers (*severely*) Some are born normal, Mr Barclay, some achieve normality. Others have to have normality thrust upon them. However, you're quite right, that is for the fairly advanced fetishist.
Martin (*still looking at the brochure*) What does one do with *that*?
Travers (*peering thoughtfully*) Ah, yes—that. You know I haven't the foggiest idea. Our man in Copenhagen bought a gross of them but the instructions are all in Japanese so we shall have to wait and see. We're enlarging our range all the time, you see, trying to appeal to a wider public. We hope that our shops will become the sort of place a man will want to bring his mother.
Martin Even a man without an Oedipus complex!
Travers But we're not here just to make money you know. We provide a *service*. Now *you* have the honour of being our figurehead, our symbol, as it were. And we welcome you. Miss Winters is marvellous, of course, but since her poor husband died we have rather lacked—the—er—rough male thrust of conquest.
Martin Her husband; didn't he, as it were, give his life to the cause?
Travers (*lyrically*) Ah, there was a dedicated man! (*He indicates hidden merchandise*) Killed himself selling these to the Venezuelan police. They thought they were truncheons. Now, you must see our library . . .

Martin Library? I thought they were just dirty books.

Travers (*pained*) Please, Mr Barclay, watch your language. We regard our library as the fountain of new knowledge, washing away the dark shadows of inhibition; windows on a new world, a glimpse of the sunny uplands of erotic liberation. (*Pause*) Then again *some* of our books *are*—as you suggest—perfectly filthy.

Martin (*seriously*) Mr Travers, I'm beginning to wonder if I'm your man. At one brief moment in my career I did acquire a certain reputation as prosecuting counsel in Lord Carbridge's anti-porn case. I was known, for a short, rather jocular period at the Bar, as "The Scourge of Soho".

Travers Splendid! Splendid! You have crossed the floor of the House! Seen the light! We can build on that. "Eminent lawyer admits, 'I can see nothing wrong in Sex'."

Martin Oh Lord, what have I let myself in for?

Travers About five years, if things go wrong. But you mustn't worry. Try to look upon it as a crusade—a service to mankind. Now, let me show you our new Bondage department.

Travers leads the way out through the office

The Lights fade, and come up on Area 2

SCENE 4

Six months later

Bill and Helen come out of the lift. Bill wears a large, sad blue rosette

Bill Oh Helen, it's not that I lost the by-election really. It's just that not enough people actually voted for me.

Helen Cheer up, it could have happened to anybody.

Bill No, I doubt it, I'm a failure.

Helen Not at all, it takes a very special kind of man to turn a fifteen thousand majority into a lost deposit.

Bill Do you really think so? That's jolly encouraging! Do you know what I think I'll do? I think I'll offer my services to the Social Democrats.

Helen That's very sporting of you, darling—that'll help the Conservatives enormously.

Bill Yes—no—well, what else can I do?

Helen What about your old job?

Bill Cherry and I are finished. I wouldn't have the c-c-courage to ask.

Helen (*opening her flat door*) Leave it to me. I'll fix it.

Bill Sometimes I think the w-world hates me. I suppose you think I'm being paranoic?

Helen (*thoughtfully*) No. I think they really are out to get you.

Bill and Helen go into her flat

The Lights come on in the office

Travers and the Prince enter. The Prince is reading some papers

Act II, Scene 4

Prince Excellent, really excellent.
Travers (*pleased*) Thank you, sir. It's only a half-yearly trial balance sheet but it does show a truly remarkable upward trend in the business since we last saw you.
Prince Oh, first class. I think I made a good investment. I'm sorry our Chairman is in America, I would like to have congratulated him. I gather the Sex Shops came as a surprise.
Travers Yes—ah—you could say that. But he's a flexible man, he rallied. Now he's thrown himself into the business body and—ah—soul.
Prince Well, the body is appropriate.
Travers He has made some interesting innovations.
Prince That doesn't surprise me, he's an interesting man.
Travers He's expanding our library section. He's including the Encyclopaedia Britannica.
Prince Good heavens! That *does* surprise me. Has it made any difference?
Travers Well, we're getting a better class of pervert.
Prince Ah!
Travers He's actually started selling sports equipment—tennis raquets, cricket bats, etc.
Prince How is that going?
Travers Confused our regulars for a bit. They couldn't work out what to do with them.
Prince He's changing the image.
Travers Yes. Our displays are much more subtle. Erotic perfumes, see-through track suits, candles you can actually light—and, do you know—(*surprised*)—we're even more successful.
Prince They say virtue is its own reward.
Travers Do they still? That does surprise me. Well now we have virtue *and* a twenty-five per cent increase in turnover.
Prince Excellent. I knew we had a winner in that young man. He makes a better businessman than he does a butler.
Travers (*smiling*) One man in his time plays many parts.
Prince Tell me—how is the relationship going with the managing director?
Travers Well, I'm afraid it's still highly charged, very businesslike. Tense, even.
Prince Strained.
Travers Monosyllabic.
Prince They don't talk much.
Travers Almost never. Send each other little notes like: "Gone to New York—back in four days" and "Pray let me have your views on half a sheet of paper". (*Vaguely*) Personally, I've never held very strong views on half a sheet of paper ...
Prince Distant.
Travers Oh, *continents* apart. In fact, he's in South America at the moment.
Prince I feel somehow responsible, you know.
Travers For South America?
Prince No, for their break-up. I wish there was something I could do.
Travers It's pride of course that's keeping them apart. But she's meeting

him at the airport tonight, so I have reason to believe that we may be on the verge of reconciliation.

Prince Splendid!

Travers Yesterday he sent her a cable saying, "Flying home—terribly sorry—I've been a fool."

Prince And what do you suppose he meant by that?

Travers Well, I think it must refer to their private lives—unless he's having misgivings about trying to sell plastic bananas to the Brazilians.

Prince Tell me, is his law practice suffering much?

Travers I gather he is not too popular in his chambers or with Lord Temple.

Cherry bustles into the office, and through into the flat turning on lights

Cherry He's not too popular with me either. Do come in and have a drink.

Prince Why is that?

Travers pours drinks. Cherry closes the curtains

Cherry Because I never *see* him. He goes straight from the office to his own nasty little flat nowadays. Six months ago he drove me mad proposing to me every day.

The Prince and Cherry sit on the sofa

Prince (*leering slightly*) What did he propose?

Cherry Now he's always rushing round the world and his only propositions are business ones. *Very* boring. (*Smiling self-consciously*) Still I'm glad to say he's coming home at last.

Travers (*beaming*) But isn't it lovely being so successful. Wine, women and song.

Travers hands them drinks, collects his own then sits in the armchair

Prince (*eyebrows raised*) I somehow never saw you in that light before.

Travers (*seriously*) It was many years before I discovered the discos—Tramp, Annabel's, Wedgie's ... Much of my—er—bolt was, as it were, shot. Wasted years. (*He yawns*)

Prince Is that why you are so tired?

Travers No—I only go on a rave up on Fridays and Saturdays. It's only just that we've got a lot on, as you know, and we're a little understaffed. It's the travelling that's killing me. So confusing.

The telephone rings

Cherry Hello? ... Oh, hello, Helen ... How are you? ... You are? ... Well I'm not surprised ... What, lost his deposit! ... Poor Bill ... And poor you ... What now? ... Well, it's not awfully convenient, you see I'm going out to dinner, then I'm meeting Martin at the airport ... Yes, then I think we're going on to Sussex ... Well, okay, if it's only for a moment, but don't think me rude if I'm rushing ...' Bye. (*She rings off*) Hmm. (*To Travers*) Bill has failed to get in at his by-election and Helen, I think, plans to offload him back on us.

Act II, Scene 4

Travers Good chap, Bill. Bit thick but good at the travelling. (*He dozes off in his chair*)

Helen comes out of her door and rings Cherry's bell

Cherry opens the door

Helen Cherry!
Cherry Oh, hello, Helen. (*She turns to the Prince*) Can I introduce Prince Hassan?
Helen (*as near animation as she ever gets*) Ooh, yes!
Cherry Miss Temple.

The Prince kisses Helen's hand, and she is obviously impressed

Helen How do you do? What do I call you?
Prince (*holding her hand in his two and exuding oriental charm*) Oh Bertie, please.
Cherry And you know Mr Travers, of course. Oh, never mind.

Travers is asleep, and Helen and the Prince look into each other's eyes

Helen So sorry to barge in. Do hope I'm not interrupting.
Prince (*breathing it*) Not at all, Helen. I'm just waiting to take Cherry out for a brief supper before she deserts me for her rural retreat. Do carry on with your—er—problem.
Helen (*tearing herself away from the Prince*) Well, it's Bill. He's driving me potty. I wondered if you could find him a job again? Preferably abroad.
Cherry I don't see why not. (*She turns to Travers*) What do you think, Mr T.? (*Travers still sleeps*) Never mind. Martin's doing much too much travelling and Travers is worn out.
Helen You could see more of Martin and I could see less of Bill.
Cherry Right—you're on. (*She holds out her hand*)
Helen (*shaking it and smiling*) You're angelic, thank you.

Travers suddenly wakes up

Travers Good Heavens—I nearly forgot. I've got that new delivery from Hong Kong to show you.
Cherry Not now, please, Cedric. Won't it wait?
Travers (*already going towards the office door*) Sorry I must have your comments before tomorrow. It's a bit "way out" but it could be a big seller. Won't take long.

Travers exits through the office

Helen (*gloomily*) Well I suppose I must get back to the pre-marital bliss.
Prince You don't sound very excited. Is there something lacking in your choice of mate?
Helen Well he's not a very choice mate. It's a sort of love-hate relationship without the love.
Cherry Helen, as I'm not going to be here, why don't you stay, stay here until Bill gets tired and goes home?

Helen But you know Bill, he'll stay all night.
Cherry That's all right, stay the night, I won't be here.
Helen How kind of you, darling, thank you.
Cherry Now I must go and tidy up. The sofa makes up into a bed. Oh, you know how everything works . . . (*She picks up a wrapped parcel from the shelf*) Oh, I bought Martin a welcome home present—see what you think. (*She gives the box to Helen*) He always was a bit bad on times.

Cherry exits to the bathroom

Helen And places—you should have bought him a compass.
Prince (*opening the box to reveal a watch*) What a nice watch—and so simple.
Helen I like just simple platinum and diamonds.
Prince Now we must get you fixed up. What's all this about a bed?
Helen I think you pull something here.
Prince Oh I see—I'm sorry to hear about your boy friend's election defeat.

They start opening the sofa into a bed

Helen Are you interested in politics?
Prince I have to be. You could almost say I *am* politics in my country.
Helen (*impressed*) How super. Do you have elections?
Prince Not exactly. I don't think we're quite ready for democracy. We have sort of eliminating rounds.

During the above Helen and the Prince make up the sofa-bed. Finally, having finished they sit on each edge of the bed and the Prince turns on the charm

(*Doing what is expected of him*) So you're a beautiful single lady who is bored with her boy friend?
Helen (*giggling*) Yes—isn't it *awful*.
Prince Perhaps you will come and visit me one day. I have a summer house by the sea. The sand is dead white and the sea dark blue—great grey dolphins play around my yacht, which lies at anchor off the palm-fringed shore . . .
Helen Sounds all right. But I'm not quite sure where your country is?
Prince Bugger my country. I'm talking about the Seychelles.
Helen (*after a pause*) Not quite sure where they are either.
Prince It doesn't matter. I will send my private jet for you.
Helen Super.
Prince Perhaps we can discuss it over luncheon tomorrow. My hotel—one o'clock.
Helen Which hotel?
Prince The one I bought last week. The Ali Hassan—it used to be called Claridges.
Helen (*blankly*) Oh, that one.
Prince I'll send my car for you. All right?
Helen (*a little more enthusiastically*) All right.

Cherry enters, with a suitcase

Act II, Scene 4   51

Cherry Ready at last.
Helen I think I'm into a sort of white slavers' mystery tour. Still as long as it's first-class.
Cherry Bertie, I think we ought to go, if you don't mind.

The Prince takes her suitcase and moves towards the door

Helen, help yourself to everything.
Helen Thanks a million. It's going to be a long siege. Goodnight.
Prince Until tomorrow.
Helen Ooh, yes.
Cherry 'Bye.

Cherry and the Prince exit and go down in the lift

Just as they enter the lift Helen catches sight of the watch, picks it up and goes towards the door

Helen Oh, you forgot Martin's . . . Oh, well . . . (*She opens up the sofa bed and bounces on it once or twice*)

Helen disappears into the bathroom where she quickly slips off her dress. Bill comes out of Helen's front door, opposite, and puts his ear to Cherry's front door keyhole. He almost knocks, then changes his mind and goes back into Helen's flat. Helen emerges from the bathroom in bra and pants

The telephone rings. Helen answers it

Helen (*on the telephone*) Hallo . . . Oh, it's you . . . I thought it would be . . . It depends how you look at it . . . Well, the good news is you can have your old job back . . . Not at all. The bad news is, and it's not easy to put this, but our affair is over—good-bye. (*She replaces the receiver. To herself*) I think I put it rather well. (*She leaves the telephone off the hook, turns off the main lights and gets into bed, leaving only the bedside light on. She yawns, puts cotton wool earplugs into her ears, and turns off the lamp*)

Music link

Martin comes out of the lift. He carries a suitcase and an airline bag. He is obviously very weary. He almost goes into Helen's door then remembers in time, and smiles to himself. He unlocks Cherry's door and lets himself in

The room is in almost total darkness so we hardly see him put down his bag and slip off some of his clothes. He sits on the bed to remove his shoes and we hear a sudden squeak and Helen switches on the lamp and glares at Martin. Martin is amazed. They both try and cover themselves with the sheet

Martin What are you doing here?
Helen What?
Martin I said what are you doing here?
Helen You'll have to speak up, I can't hear. (*She remembers the earplugs*) Oh! (*She takes them out*)
Martin (*shouting*) Never mind! Where's Cherry?

Helen There's no need to shout. She's gone to the country. She let me stay here to get away from Bill.
Martin Ah, I see. Where is he?
Helen He's in my flat.
Martin Does he know you're here?
Helen Yes, he's telephoned.
Martin (*beginning to get dressed in a panic*) My God, he could come in any moment.
Helen Yes.
Martin He'd never believe this.
Helen No.
Martin (*wildly*) He'll come and hit me, I know he will. Quick, my clothes!

Bill comes out of Helen's flat and bangs on Cherry's door

Bill Helen. I know you're in there. Open the door!

Martin and Helen freeze in horror. Bill bangs on the door

Look, I've got to talk to you. I've tried 'phoning, but I can't get any answer—please answer.
Helen (*pretending to be sleepy*) I'm asleep. Go away.
Bill If you don't open this door at once I'll break it down.

In a flash Martin is under the bed. Helen throws his clothes after him. Bill hammers on the door again

Helen All right, I'm coming. (*She turns on the main lights*)

Bill takes a small run at the door. Just as he hurls himself at it, Helen opens it and he charges into the room, out of control

Bill (*very angrily*) About t-t-t- ...
Helen (*helpfully*) Turn?
Bill (*shouting*) T-t-time. W-what are you doing here? You're in bed.
Helen It's a fairly reasonable place to try and get some sleep.
Bill B-but ... (*He looks around him wildly*) There's a man, isn't there? You've got a man here!
Helen (*after a moment's pause*) A man—where? Of course I haven't. No such luck.
Bill You're a loose woman, Helen. I always knew it. He'll be under the bed.
Helen Ridiculous! Under the bed, indeed.

Everything now happens at once. Bill leaps forward to fold the bed

Mr Travers bursts in from the office and the Prince and Cherry are seen coming out of the lift

As Bill folds up the bed, Helen is thrown in a half-naked heap on top of Martin. Travers stands with a handful of chains and a huge whip from the bondage department, wearing a leather jacket and shorts

Travers (*waving his whip*) It's the new consignment from Hong Kong, you like it, don't you? You love it. Admit that you *love* it! (*He advances menacingly on them, cracking his whip*)

Act II, Scene 4

At this moment Cherry enters the flat. She stands by the door taking in this amazing scene

Cherry Good heavens!

They all turn and look at her

(*After a long pause, very matter-of-fact*) Is this a private orgy or can anyone join in? And that, I take it, is the new consignment from Hong Kong, Cedric. Very fetching.
Bill Forget Cedric. Look at them ... caught in the act. Decadent, shameless! I'm speechless. I'm leaving.
Helen Martin came back early—he thought I was you in the bed ...
Bill Speechless!
Helen Excuse me—I think I'm going to faint.

Helen runs out of the flat and falls straight into the Prince's arms who helps her into her flat

Bill Oh, Helen.
Travers Back man! You've gone far enough.
Bill Me! I never touched her!
Travers Quite so, far enough. (*He brandishes his whip*) Into the office young man, and we will discuss your future with Pleasure and Leisure, and be quick about it or I'll whip you!
Bill Oh would you really—thank you very much!

Bill and Travers exit through the office

Martin and Cherry are left alone in the flat

Cherry Well?
Martin Appearances can be deceptive.
Cherry Is that all you've got to say?
Martin No. (*Matter-of-factly*) I spoke to Hardacre in New York. He thinks we should open a branch in Buffalo.
Cherry I see. (*Playing his game*) We could send Bill over to manage it.
Martin Hmm. "Buffalo Bill"—good idea—as long as I don't have to do any more travelling.
Cherry I was thinking of taking a short trip.
Martin Really?
Cherry Yes. Somewhere suitably romantic—for a honeymoon.
Martin (*shocked*) Honeymoon! (*Trying to be cool*) Er—anyone I know?
Cherry (*casually*) I was wondering what you were doing—for the next twenty or thirty years?
Martin Me! (*Patting his shorts*) Well—er—I haven't got my diary on me—but I think something could be arranged!

Martin and Cherry smile at each other, as—

the CURTAIN falls

The CURTAIN *rises again, to show them embracing*

FURNITURE AND PROPERTY LIST

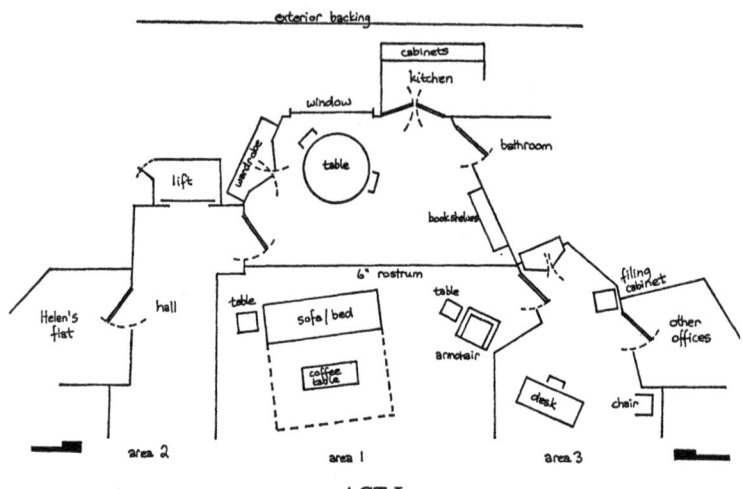

ACT I

On stage: LIVING-ROOM:
Sofa/bed with bedding and cushions
Bed table. *On it:* lamp, alarm clock
Small circular table
2 small chairs
Armchair
Occasional table. *On it:* ashtray
Bookshelves. *In them:* books. *Below them:* cupboard. *On top and inside cupboard:* various drinks including whisky, gin, jug of water, soda syphon, empty bottle, assorted glasses, silver salver, lighter, telephone, ashtray, stereo cassette-player
Coffee-table. *On it:* ashtray
In wardrobe: **Cherry**'s evening dress, fur coat
Carpet
Curtains closed

OFFICE:
Desk. *On it:* writing materials, blotter, telephone. *In drawers:* files, box file containing wig and moustache
Desk chair
Small chair
Filing cabinet

CORRIDOR:
Practical bells on front doors of both flats

Caught in the Act 55

Off stage: File of papers, brochure (**Travers**)
Heavy suitcase (**Bill**)
Coffee tray. *On it:* 2 cups of coffee, 2 saucers, 2 teaspoons, cream jug, sugar basin
Bunch of roses, bottle of champagne (**Martin**)
Teddy-bear (**Helen**)
Vase (**Cherry**)
Used dishes and cutlery for two (set during Black-out)
Milk carton, newspaper (set in corridor during Black-out)
Bunch of roses, bottle of champagne (**Martin**)
Ice bucket, vase (**Martin**)
Towel, toothbrush with paste (**Cherry**)
Make-up (**Cherry**)
Box of Kleenex (**Cherry**)
Bunch of roses, bottle of champagne (**Prince**)

Personal: **Martin:** key, wallet, watch, spectacles
Helen: engagement ring, handbag with latchkey
Cherry: engagement ring, key
Prince: watch

ACT II

Set: **Martin's** suitcase in wardrobe cupboard
Wristwatch in wrapped parcel—concealed from sight on drinks shelf

Off stage: 2 champagne glasses (**Martin**)
Chamber pot (**Martin**)
Bottle of champagne, 2 glasses (**Martin**)
Glass of brandy, cigar (**Martin**)
File of documents, brochure (**Travers**)
Briefcase containing 3 copies of long document (**Travers**)
Suitcase (**Cherry**)
Ear plugs (**Helen**)
Suitcase, air-line bag (**Martin**)
Chains, whip (**Travers**)

Personal: **Prince:** gold cigarette case, cane
Bill: notes, blue rosette
Travers: watch, sun glasses

LIGHTING PLOT

Director's Note: Whenever possible, at the end of scenes there should be a cross-fade, and not a dead Black-out. The time element can be indicated by a short musical link

Property fittings required: hall light, lift light, wall brackets, bed lamp, office light
Interior composite set: corridor, living-room, office. The same scene throughout

ACT I

To open: Night. Bed lamp on, corridor light on

Cue 1	**Travers** switches on office light *Snap on office lighting*	(Page 1)
Cue 2	**Travers** switches off office light *Snap off office lighting*	(Page 2)
Cue 3	**Cherry** switches off bed lamp *Snap off bed lamp—room in darkness. Dim corridor lighting*	(Page 2)
Cue 4	At end of "intimacy" music *Bring up dawn effect*	(Page 3)
Cue 5	**Cherry** opens curtains *Brighten overall lighting, except for office*	(Page 3)
Cue 6	**Cherry** exits to bathroom *Bring up office lighting: day*	(Page 14)
Cue 7	**Travers** exits *Fade to Black-out, then bring up living-room and corridor lighting: day*	(Page 14)
Cue 8	**Cherry:** "I'll drink to that!" *Fade to Black-out, then bring up corridor lighting*	(Page 18)
Cue 9	**Helen** and **Bill** enter **Helen's** flat *Fade to Black-out, then bring up living-room lighting*	(Page 18)
Cue 10	**Martin** and **Cherry** embrace *Cross-fade to corridor lighting*	(Page 19)
Cue 11	**Helen** and **Bill** exit *Cross-fade to living-room*	(Page 19)
Cue 12	**Martin** and **Cherry** exit to kitchen *Cross-fade to office lighting*	(Page 21)
Cue 13	**Bill** exits after **Travers** *Cross-fade to living-room and corridor lighting: evening, brackets and lamp on*	(Page 22)

Cue 14	**Martin** turns down lights *Snap off brackets*	(Page 23)
Cue 15	**Cherry** turns up one bracket *Snap on one bracket and covering spots*	(Page 23)
Cue 16	**Cherry** turns up second bracket *Bring up second bracket and full living-room lighting*	(Page 24)

ACT II

To open:	As close of previous Act	
Cue 17	**Martin** starts to clean up living-room *Fade living-room lighting; retain corridor*	(Page 34)
Cue 18	**Helen** exits into her flat *Cross-fade to living-room lighting; night*	(Page 35)
Cue 19	**Travers** switches on office light *Snap on office lighting*	(Page 35)
Cue 20	**Cherry** switches off office light *Snap off office lighting*	(Page 36)
Cue 21	**Martin:** "Good night, Ms Chairperson." *Fade to Black-out, then bring up office lighting: day*	(Page 38)
Cue 22	**Martin** enters from lift *Bring up overall lighting in corridor and living-room: day*	(Page 40)
Cue 23	As **Travers** exits through office *Fade to Black-out, then bring up corridor lighting*	(Page 46)
Cue 24	**Bill** and **Helen** exit *Bring up office lighting: night*	(Page 46)
Cue 25	**Cherry** goes into living-room *Bring up living-room lighting: night, lamp and brackets on*	(Page 48)
Cue 26	**Helen** turns off brackets *Snap off brackets, retain bed lamp. Dim office and corridor*	(Page 51)
Cue 27	**Helen** switches off bed lamp *Snap off bed lamp*	(Page 51)
Cue 28	**Helen** switches on bed lamp *Snap on bed lamp*	(Page 51)
Cue 29	**Helen** switches on brackets *Snap on full night lighting in living-room*	(Page 52)

EFFECTS PLOT

ACT I

Cue 1	As dawn lighting fades up *Alarm clock rings*	(Page 3)
Cue 2	**Cherry:** ". . . with you in a minute." *Living-room telephone rings*	(Page 14)
Cue 3	**Martin:** "Anyone home?" *Living-room telephone rings*	(Page 23)
Cue 4	**Martin** turns on stereo *Sweet music*	(Page 23)
Cue 5	**Cherry** turns off music *Cut sweet music*	(Page 24)

ACT II

Cue 6	**Helen:** ". . . aggressive spirit, you must admit." *Living-room telephone rings*	(Page 32)
Cue 7	As Scene 3 opens *Office telephone rings*	(Page 38)
Cue 8	**Travers** replaces receiver *Office telephone rings again*	(Page 38)
Cue 9	**Prince:** ". . . the elusive folder—interesting." *Office telephone rings*	(Page 42)
Cue 10	**Travers:** "So confusing." *Living-room telephone rings*	(Page 48)
Cue 11	**Helen** enters from bathroom *Living-room telephone rings*	(Page 51)

MADE AND PRINTED IN GREAT BRITAIN BY
LATIMER TREND & COMPANY LTD PLYMOUTH
MADE IN ENGLAND

www.ingramcontent.com/pod-product-compliance
Ingram Content Group UK Ltd.
Pitfield, Milton Keynes, MK11 3LW, UK
UKHW021847210426
5322IPUK00022B/518